Contents

Introduction

Insight into PET is for students who are going to take the Cambridge PET exam. It's an intensive exam preparation course, whose aim is to help students develop the skills they'll need for success in the exam.

How is the book organised?

Insight into PET follows the organisation of the exam. There are four chapters, Reading, Writing, Listening and Speaking, containing a total of 35 short units. Each unit works systematically through one part of the exam, building up students' confidence and their ability to do the different tasks. The work on each part ends with an exam practice exercise in examination format.

There are tapes/CDs to accompany the book.

The book also contains:
- Supplementary Activities for each unit
- a separate Grammar File with exercises
- a complete Practice Test
- the recording script
- information about the marking of the Writing and Speaking Tests

How can the book be used?

The book contains enough material for approximately 50 hours. Each unit provides work for one 50–60 minute lesson. Teachers can choose to work systematically through each chapter, or select units to match their students' needs.

Overview of the PET exam

Paper	Name	Timing	Content
Paper 1	Reading/ Writing	1 hour 30 minutes	**Reading:** Five parts which test a range of reading skills with a variety of texts, from very short notices to longer texts. **Writing:** Three parts which test writing skills ranging from producing variations on simple sentences to a 100-word piece of continuous writing.
Paper 2	Listening	30 minutes (approx)	Four parts ranging from short exchanges to longer dialogues and monologues.
Paper 3	Speaking	10–12 mins per pair of candidates	Four parts which include asking and answering questions, discussing with a partner, talking about a picture and expressing opinions.

Reading

In the exam

In Part 1 of the Reading Test, you will read five short notices, labels, notes, messages, postcards or emails and answer a multiple-choice question on each one.

In this unit

- Different words, same meaning
- Introduction to multiple-choice
- Writing notices

To start you thinking … about notices

1 Look at these labels and notices. In pairs, decide what they're connected with. Write the letter under the correct heading below.

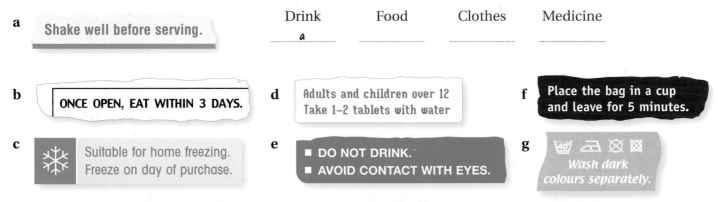

a **Shake well before serving.**

Drink	Food	Clothes	Medicine
a			

b **ONCE OPEN, EAT WITHIN 3 DAYS.**

c ❄ Suitable for home freezing. Freeze on day of purchase.

d Adults and children over 12 Take 1–2 tablets with water

e ■ DO NOT DRINK. ■ AVOID CONTACT WITH EYES.

f **Place the bag in a cup and leave for 5 minutes.**

g *Wash dark colours separately.*

Different words, same meaning

2 For multiple-choice questions, you need to understand that the same information can be expressed in different ways.

e.g. Keep closed   is the same as   Never leave open
     Smoking is forbidden is the same as   You're not allowed to smoke

Complete these sentences with one or two words so that the second sentence means the same as the first.

a Not suitable for use on plastic surfaces. = ... use on plastic surfaces.
b Keep medicine out of reach of children. = Make sure children .... get the medicine.
c Don't walk on the grass. = Keep .... the grass.
d No entry without permit. = You can't enter if you .... have a permit.
   = Only people .... permits can enter.
e Maximum capacity 50 passengers. = No .... than 50 passengers allowed.
   = Up .... 50 passengers only.
f Not to be given to children under 12. = You .... give it to children of less than 12 years of age.
g Closed until 8.00 am. = The shop will be open .... 8.00 am.
h Low ceiling. Mind your head. = Be .... because the ceiling is low.

6

Introduction to multiple-choice

3 Read these notices.

First answer the questions in *italics* for each notice – they'll help you choose the correct multiple-choice answer. (Questions 1–2 have only two choices and Questions 3–4 have three choices.) Circle the correct answer.

1
Important: Please read the instruction book before using the machine.

*Do you **have** to use the instruction book, or is it just a good idea?*

   A This machine cannot be used without the instruction book.
   B This machine should only be used after you've read the instruction book.

2
Please switch off the lights and lock the door when you leave.

Which action must you do first when leaving?

   A Before leaving, turn the lights off.
   B Before leaving, lock the door.

3
No entry except with a valid permit which can be bought from the Town Hall.

Why would you go to the Town Hall?

   A If you want to come in, you must have a permit.
   B You must go to the Town Hall if you have a permit.
   C You need a permit if you want to enter the Town Hall.

4
Accident here at 6.00 pm on Sunday 25th September. Please contact police on 3569087 if you saw anything.

Who do the police want to speak to?

   A The police would like to speak to people on September 25th.
   B The police want to speak to people who had an accident on September 25th.
   C The police want people to tell them if they saw the accident on September 25th.

Writing notices

4 This is the story of Sam Podd who doesn't read notices and messages.
This sometimes causes problems for him – and for other people too. Read the story.
In pairs, write the notices and messages that Sam didn't read.

   a This morning on the bus, Sam tried to talk to the bus driver but the driver said, 'Sorry, can't talk when I'm driving,' and pointed to the notice which said:

   b When Sam tried to use the lift to go up to his office, the 20 people already standing in the lift wouldn't let him in. Sam hadn't read the notice which said:

   c At lunchtime, in a bookshop, Sam fell down a small step because he didn't see the notice that said:

   d 'My wife is out late tonight. Where is she?' thought Sam. He didn't see the note from his wife that was on the table:

➜ See page 92 for Supplementary Activities. More message practice in Unit 2.

Reading

In the exam

In Part 1 of the Reading Test, you will read five short notices, labels, notes, messages, postcards or emails and answer a multiple-choice question on each one.

In this unit

- What's on the notice board?
- Practice with multiple-choice questions
- Exam practice for Part 1

To start you thinking … about making contact

1 **How many different ways are there of making contact with someone? Write as many as you can in one minute.**

e.g. *a letter*

Compare your ideas with a partner.

Which way do you think is the easiest?
Which do you use least often?
Which do you most enjoy receiving?

What's on the notice board?

2 **All these notices and messages are on a college notice board. Read them quickly and then write the number of the notice after a–f.**

a You want to contact a student who used to be in your class. 7
b You have found a bag in the ladies' toilets. ....
c You don't understand the new Word for Windows computer programme. ....
d You need to earn some money, but not on Saturday or Sunday. ....
e You want to take some exercise in the evenings. ....
f You need to know where your class will be. ....

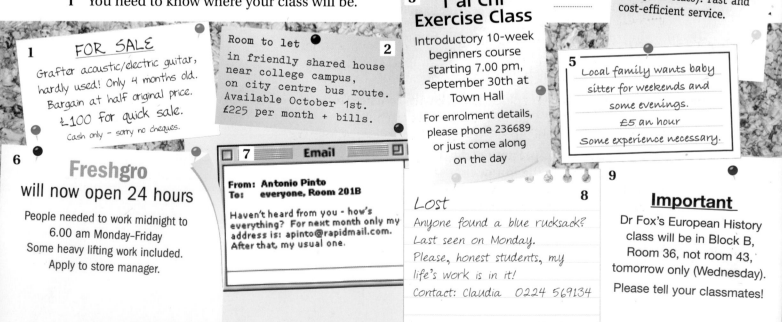

4
Computer problems
IT support for home computers. We can provide hardware/software support for almost all models of PCs (sorry, no Macs). Fast and cost-efficient service.

1
FOR SALE
Grafter acoustic/electric guitar, hardly used! Only 4 months old. Bargain at half original price.
£100 for quick sale.
Cash only – sorry no cheques.

2
Room to let
in friendly shared house near college campus, on city centre bus route. Available October 1st. £225 per month + bills.

3
T'ai Chi Exercise Class
Introductory 10-week beginners course starting 7.00 pm, September 30th at Town Hall
For enrolment details, please phone 236689 or just come along on the day

5
Local family wants baby sitter for weekends and some evenings.
£5 an hour
Some experience necessary.

6
Freshgro
will now open 24 hours
People needed to work midnight to 6.00 am Monday–Friday
Some heavy lifting work included.
Apply to store manager.

7 Email
From: Antonio Pinto
To: everyone, Room 201B
Haven't heard from you – how's everything? For next month only my address is: apinto@rapidmail.com. After that, my usual one.

8
Lost
Anyone found a blue rucksack? Last seen on Monday. Please, honest students, my life's work is in it! Contact: Claudia 0224 569134

9
Important
Dr Fox's European History class will be in Block B, Room 36, not room 43, tomorrow only (Wednesday).
Please tell your classmates!

In the exam it's important that you understand what the notice or message is saying *before* you answer the multiple-choice question. Read notices 1–9 again.

In pairs, discuss your answers to these questions.

Notice 1 Why is the seller asking such a low price?
Notice 2 Will the accommodation cost more than £225 per month? Why?
Notice 3 To join a class, is it necessary to telephone first?
Notice 4 Why would you be interested in this service?
Notice 5 What is an important thing for the advertiser?
Notice 6 Why are Freshgro advertising?
Notice 7 Why is Antonio sending this email address?
Notice 8 What is Claudia's 'life's work'?
Notice 9 Where will Dr Fox's European History class be on Friday?

Practice with multiple-choice questions

3 Answer these multiple-choice questions about the notices and messages.

Notice 1 A The seller wants to get some cash quickly.
  B The seller has played his guitar a lot.
  C The seller is hoping to get more than £100 for the guitar.

Notice 2 How much will this accommodation cost?
  A £225 per month
  B £225 per month plus bus fares
  C More than £225 per month

Notice 3 A It's important to reserve your place in advance.
  B It's not necessary to reserve your place.
  C You must reserve your place on the day.

Notice 4 You might be interested in this service if you
  A have a Mac computer which sometimes has problems.
  B sometimes have difficulty using your PC.
  C want to buy some new software from this company.

Notice 5 A To do this job you must like babies very much.
  B If you want the job, you must have done babysitting before.
  C You have to be free every evening for this job.

Notice 6 A Freshgro is looking for a store manager
  B There are problems for people who work at Freshgro.
  C Freshgro have increased their opening hours.

Notice 7 A Antonio wants his friends to know how to contact him.
  B Antonio's friends must write to him this month.
  C Antonio thinks his friends have lost his address.

Notice 8 A Claudia wants her rucksack back with or without the things inside.
  B Claudia is afraid that not all students are honest.
  C Claudia is worried about losing all her notes and papers.

Notice 9 Dr Fox's European History class will
  A no longer be on Wednesday.
  B be in a different room from now on.
  C change rooms for tomorrow.

➡ See page 92 for Supplementary Activities.
See page 10 for Exam practice for Part 1.

Exam practice for Part 1

Exam tip

- Read the short message, notice, etc. Think about what it's saying *before* you look at the A, B, C choices.

Look at the text in each question.
What does it say?
Mark the correct letter – A, B or C.

Example:

0

WARNING
CCTV cameras in use in
and around this building

(A) This area is guarded by cameras.

B Cameras are useful here.

C Be careful with cameras around here.

1

Computer World
Discounts for students only
with student cards.
Ask inside for details.

A If you show your student card, they'll give you details.

B You can't get reduced prices without your student card.

C If you go inside, they'll give you a student card.

2

☎ MESSAGE

To: Pierre

From: Xavier

Pierre – no seats on any Paris flight on Sunday. There's space on Monday's 09.00, but you must confirm before tomorrow lunchtime.

A Pierre's flight has been changed.

B It's possible for Pierre to fly tomorrow.

C Pierre's flight has not yet been reserved.

3

> **Moving house?**
>
> Don't forget to tell us so we can keep you on our mailing list.
>
> Complete your new details on this form and return it to us.

A Remember to complete the mailing list.

B We'd like you to send us your new address.

C The details of our mailing list are on the form.

4

> Chris
> Gone to Dad's. He rang in a panic – he could smell gas! Dinner's in the oven – start without me. Back soon
> Angie

A Angie went out because of a phone call.

B Angie's father rang to warn her about something.

C Chris will have to make his own dinner.

5

> If you are not satisfied with your purchase, please feel free to return it to any of our branches. We are happy to exchange or refund the cost of any unused item.

If you don't want to keep what you've bought,

A you must not use it before returning it.

B you have to change it for something else.

C you should take it back to where you bought it.

Reading

In the exam

In Part 2 of the Reading Test, you will read descriptions of five people, followed by eight short texts. You then 'match' the five people to five of the texts.

In this unit

- Matching practice – pictures to text
- Finding the information quickly

To start you thinking … about people

1 Look at these pictures. How old do you think the people are? What do you think they're thinking about?

Davina   Karen   Richard   Thomas   Maddy

Matching practice – pictures to text

2 In the exam you have to match *descriptions* of people to short texts. In this exercise, you have to match *pictures* of people to the texts.

Read what these four people say about their lives. In pairs, discuss your answers to the question after each one. Then match each text to one of the pictures in exercise 1 (there is one extra picture).

Text 1

Since we had Molly eight months ago the thing that's changed is our sleeping. Sometimes I sit at our kitchen table and dream of eight hours' uninterrupted sleep. I guess the time will come when she won't wake us up anymore. People say the first five years are the worst, but then my mother told me you can't relax until they're 18. Eeek!

   a What's the most difficult thing in this person's life at the moment?

   b Match: Picture of ....

Text 2

Well, at the moment I'm doing about five kilometres, three times a week. The race is in about three months – I'm really worried about it because I've never run 40 kilometres before but I'm following a training programme specially for the over-50s, and I'm not doing it alone – one of my colleagues from work is doing it with me. He's a bit older than me, so if he can do it, so can I.

   c Is this person more worried because of age or the activity they're going to do?

   d Match: Picture of ....

Text 3

I hope that I'll be managing director of the company in ten years' time. I'm ambitious and good at what I do. I expect to be promoted to department head at the end of this year – if I'm not, I'll move to some other organisation that recognises my abilities. Or maybe I'll even start my own company. Whatever happens, I'm determined to succeed.

   e What do you think about this person's chances of success?

   f Match: Picture of ....

Text 4

We've been going out for about three years, on and off, and we're planning to get married next year. People say we're a bit young, and it's true there's lots we still want to do – finish studying, travel, live abroad, try new things, but we can do them together. And we're not going to have a traditional wedding – we're planning something a bit special.

   g How much change does this person think marriage will bring to their lives?

   h Match: Picture of ....

Finding the information quickly

3 In the exam, you have a lot to do in a short time. Allow about ten minutes for this exercise. You're going to read about six different places where people can have an unusual wedding ceremony. As you're reading, answer questions 1–7.

1 If you like being up in the air, which ceremonies would be attractive?

2 Which might appeal to people who enjoy the world of show business?

3 At which places are animals part of the holiday?

4 Which places mention the time of day or year as important?

5 At which places can you get some sort of souvenir of the event?

6 Which would be quickest to arrange?

7 Which one involves getting wet?

WEDDING BELLS
WITH A DIFFERENCE

A *New Zealand*

If you want to say "I do" while jumping off a bridge together this is the place for you. Believe it or not, a bungee jumping wedding is first choice for some couples. The jump, T-shirts and a video to show everyone back at home are all included in the price, which is much lower than you might expect. Or you could just have a quiet ceremony overlooking the hot springs at Rotorua.

B *Las Vegas, USA*

Las Vegas, the world's wedding capital, has a wedding every 5 minutes and 17 seconds. And that's what it's famous for – quick ceremonies without much paperwork or formalities. But if you want something unusual – for $100 you could hire an Elvis look-alike to walk the bride down the aisle or for a bit more you could get married above the city in a helicopter. And an evening in the famous casinos is not to be missed – you might start married life a lot richer!

C *Disney World, Florida*

As you'd expect, this is fantasy land. Your marriage could be on the set of *Aladdin* or *Beauty and the Beast* and you could arrive in Cinderella's glass carriage drawn by white horses. You can even get Mickey Mouse to sign the wedding certificate. And they will make a film of your special day, with your names there as the stars. All this in temperatures over 30°C, too. But one word of warning – it's not cheap.

D *Key Largo, Florida*

Here couples and their guests (but not too many for practical reasons) get married underwater in wet suits. Tropical fish take no notice – they've seen it all before. Bride and groom, and their guests, have to take a diving course before at a cost of about $195 each. And in the evening, take off your wet suits and enjoy the wide variety of entertainment in the resort.

E *Lapland*

Stay at the Ice Hotel in Jukkasjarvi which has its own ice chapel. You can travel there by sleigh pulled by a team of husky dogs and spend your honeymoon night in a four-poster bed made of ice. The restaurant serves delicious local dishes – including reindeer and fish. Snow is guaranteed in this northern landscape, so there's plenty of skiing and other winter sports. The hotel is open from December until its walls disappear when the ice melts around May.

F *Negril, Jamaica*

A Sunset Wedding Moon package includes the opportunity to get married on a tropical beach at sunset. In the resort of Negril they specialise in weddings – in fact, it's a couples-only resort. Everything comes in twos – from his and hers water-skiing, to the Just Married T-shirts. The evenings are spent watching the sun going down or taking a gentle walk on the beach.

4 Read the descriptions of the six places again, and decide which would be the best place for the weddings of four couples (including Maddy and her fiancé from exercise 2). Put a circle round the correct choice.

1 Maddy and Darren want to get married somewhere hot, by the sea, but quiet. They're both keen on water-sports.
Place: A B C D E F

2 Raphael and Donna both love sport. They want to go with a few friends and enjoy a holiday by the sea. They want something really unusual, and their friends would like a place with lots of entertainment in the evenings.
Place: A B C D E F

3 Ulrika and Paul are planning to get married early next year. She's keen on nature and Paul doesn't like hot places. They're both interested in traditional food and ways of life.
Place: A B C D E F

4 Dimitri and Ariana are not interested in a traditional ceremony; they want something that's fun and different. They're prepared to spend quite a lot of money. They'd like a souvenir of the day to show to their future grandchildren!
Place: A B C D E F

➡ **See page 92 for Supplementary Activities. More matching practice in Unit 4.**

Which one would *you* choose, and why?

Reading

UNIT 4 Matching (2)

In the exam

In Part 2 of the Reading Test, you will read descriptions of five people, followed by eight short texts. You then 'match' the five people to five of the texts.

In this unit

- What do the people want?
- Making sure it matches
- Exam practice for Part 2

To start you thinking ... about people and places

1   Five friends – Felipe, Martina, Marcus, Emma and Josh – are all on holiday in different places.

Felipe – long distance walker, loves camping and being outdoors

Martina – loves diving in the ocean

Marcus – mad about computers, hates sport

Emma – loves cooking and entertaining friends

Josh – enjoys seeing animals and wildlife

Each person is writing a postcard to one of the others. This postcard has not been addressed and it has not been signed.
- **Who is the postcard to?**
- **Who is the postcard from?**

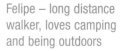

Dear ....

Wonderful place this corner of Thailand – white sandy beaches and blue seas with lots of different coloured fish and the bird life is fantastic – you see, you should have come with me! At the back of the beach there are lots of bars and restaurants. Look at the picture – see the person lying under that palm tree? That's me – I haven't moved more than 300m in a week. What a life!

Love ....

14

What do the people want?

2 In this part of the exam, you'll read about five people; each of them needs or wants a number of things. You need to understand exactly what these things are, so you know what to look for when you read the short texts.

Read about the five friends again, and the kind of books they like to read. Then complete the box below.

Felipe is interested in true stories about people who live in unusual places. He likes to know about the everyday lives they lead.

Martina loves the sea. She enjoys reading about sailing adventures, particularly modern day true stories.

Marcus enjoys science fiction stories which are believable. He doesn't read a lot so he prefers short stories which he can finish quickly.

Emma is very interested in anything to do with Far Eastern culture. She likes reading stories which people have written about their own lives. She's particularly interested in women writers.

Josh is passionate about the natural world. He enjoys reading about the way of life in the countryside – especially how it used to be in the past.

What's important for each person?

Felipe	true stories	unusual places	a
Martina	b	c	d
Marcus	e	f	g
Emma	h	i	j
Josh	k	l	m

Making sure it matches

3 You're going to choose a book for Felipe. Read these three book reviews.

A

The Island People

Daniel Turner spent ten years living on a tiny island in the middle of the Indian Ocean. He describes in fascinating detail how the inhabitants arrived on their island, and the history of their unusual language, which he learnt to speak. The book is written with intelligence and warmth.

B

Small town life

This book about the real lives of people in an ordinary town in the USA gives the big picture – the births, marriages and deaths in the community – as well as the smaller details of everyday life. For most readers, the town is probably very similar to their own, but the book is written in a way that makes it very readable.

C

THE FROZEN NORTH

The difficulties faced by the people living on the edge of the Arctic Circle are well described in this book by Sylvia Blackwood. Her style of writing is very simple but the reader gets a very clear idea, for example, of how the extreme weather is the most important influence in their daily lives. Imagine going out to do your shopping on dark days in temperatures of –30°!

Look back to what Felipe wants in exercise 2. Only one of these three books has exactly what he wants – the other two have *some* of the things he likes but not all. Read about the books again and complete the table opposite.

Which is the best book for Felipe?

Felipe. wants …	True stories ▼	Unusual places ▼	Everyday lives ▼
Book A?	✓		
Book B?			
Book C?			

→ See page 92 for Supplementary Activities.
See page 16 for Exam practice for Part 2.

Exam practice for Part 2

Exam tip

- Underline what each of the five people wants or needs (usually two or three things for each person). Some different coloured highlighter pens are useful.
- A text may look like a good match but does it have **all** the things that the person wants or needs?

The people below all want to choose a place to eat or drink.
On the opposite page there are descriptions of eight places.
Decide which place would be most suitable for the following people.
For questions 1–5, mark the correct letter (A–H).

---

1  Carlos is meeting his girlfriend Agnes in town. They don't eat meat, so they want somewhere with a really good vegetarian menu. They are both non-smokers. ☐

2  Barbara is taking her grandmother, June, out on her 70th birthday. June likes plain, simple food. She is rather deaf, and can't walk too far, but she likes being driven out into the country. ☐

3  Guy and his American colleague, Carl, want to eat after working late. Carl is interested in computers, not food, and Marcus just wants something quick. However, they both like a glass of beer with their meal. ☐

4  Julia and her friend Nevine meet every week for a good long lunch, a glass of wine, and a chat. They love seafood, and like big, lively city restaurants. ☐

5 Michael has a visitor who he wants to take out to a quiet, top-class city centre restaurant. They want to talk business. He doesn't mind paying a lot if the standard is really high. ☐

Bars and Restaurants

A

BAR 4U

You can watch the world go by through the big windows at the front of this busy city wine-bar. The menu includes a good selection of fish and seafood, and you can sit there as long as you like, even if you're only having a glass of wine.

B

This city centre Indian restaurant, occupying a cosy but rather smoky basement, offers some traditional vegetarian dishes as well as its well-known chicken and lamb specialities. Prices are reasonable, and there is a small wine list.

C

The Harvest Home

Just off the busy Cheltenham road, in the pretty village of Wibbly, this restaurant with its large car park is popular with passing motorists. One of a chain of restaurants, it serves good simple food in a friendly and relaxed atmosphere.

D

The Oasis

Take plenty of money with you if you go to this famous restaurant in the heart of the city.
The owner changed six months ago, but people say that the new owner, who trained as a chef in Paris, is just as good.

E

Loch Teen

New in town, located in a basement room, this speciality seafood bar is already quite popular. Because of the limited space, they have to have two sessions – early evening (6.30) and later (8.30) – and you might feel it's a bit rushed.

F

The Terrace Wine Bar

You can sit outside and eat under the stars here, where they serve food from midday till 3 am. The food is simple – crêpes, omelettes, pasta, burgers – and besides the good wine selection, they serve beers from over 50 countries.

G

Down to Earth

This bright, white restaurant (no smoking allowed) is situated next to the central train station.

It's vegetables only here with a whole new world of delicious and imaginative dishes.

H

Open early and late, this snack-bar is popular with both market workers and city business people. You'll only get quick and simple meals, but they'll be well cooked and quickly served. No alcohol licence.

Reading

UNIT 5 True or false? (1)

In the exam

In Part 3 of the Reading Test, you will read one long text and answer ten true or false questions.

In this unit

- Practice with short texts
- Why is it false?

To start you thinking … about animals and the natural world

1 In groups of three or four, find out if the following statements are *true* or *false*.

Someone in this group:
- has eaten insects.   **T F**
- has seen an elephant in the wild. **T F**
- is allergic to dog or cat hair. **T F**

- has more than one pet animal at the moment. **T F**
- has thought about becoming a vegetarian. **T F**
- would be happy to share a room with a snake. **T F**
- believes animals are needed for scientific research. **T F**

Practice with short texts

2 In this part of the exam, you must decide whether statements about a text are *true* or *false*.
- For a statement to be true, the information must match (but the text will use different words).
- For a statement to be false, there will be a mis-match of information (a fact may be wrong).

Look at the titles of these two short texts. What do you think you're going to read about?

Now read each text and then read the two statements that follow.
Decide which statement is true and which is false.

Dog Sitting Centre

For New Yorkers who don't want to leave their dogs in their apartments during the working day, our day-care centre is the answer.

We began our service in 1987. Today we have between 20 and 30 dogs in day-care on weekdays, from eight in the morning till eight at night, at a cost of $30. Dogs are not kept in cages, they're allowed to be free in the home and meet other dogs. There is a playroom with toys and a large colour TV – we show dog movies and cartoons. We believe that the TV creates a home environment.

SOS SHARK RESCUE

Join our campaign to stop the killing – every year over 100 million sharks die because of us – many of the sharks are hunted because their fins are used to make soup or are used in traditional medicine. This year the international Sea Life Centres are joining other organisations to try to stop this cruel and wasteful practice. Action needs to be taken now – you can help by signing up online to show your support. (Log onto www.sharktrust.org for further information.)

a You can leave your dog at the centre and go away for the weekend. **T F**

b There are different things for the dogs to do at the centre. **T F**

c Several organisations are working together to stop shark hunting. **T F**

d The campaign is asking for money. **T F**

In the *false* statements, which words make a mis-match with the information in the text? Underline them.

18

Why is it false?

3 Read the following text about a competition with a fabulous prize.

Experience Africa Competition

This is your chance to win a four-day walking safari for two people at the Phinda Private Game Reserve in South Africa, learning how to track and identify local wildlife. Simply name the animals shown here, complete the sentence in the box at the bottom of the page, and send us your entry on the form below by 31 October.

Your prize

A 4-day (three nights) walking safari in the Game Reserve. You will sleep in luxury tents for three nights and spend an extra two nights in the Phinda Mountain Lodge, with magnificent views of the Ubombo Mountains.

The 15,000 acres of Phinda, which means 'the return', is managed by the Conservation Corporation Africa (CCA). The organisation spent a long time 'returning' the area to its original wild state, and the wildlife that used to populate the area has been successfully reintroduced.

A reasonable standard of fitness is needed: each day guests can enjoy a five-hour morning walk of up to ten kilometres,

on which it is possible to spot rhinos or elephants. We may have to walk further to see different animals! Dinner is cooked for you in the camp. You will sleep in tents which are extremely comfortable.

The five-night holiday is worth from £1,690; it includes international and local return flights, meals, all wildlife activities, local drinks and safari laundry. Airport taxes and travel insurance are not included.

So, identify these animals, fill in your entry form and you could be the lucky winner. But remember, prizes must be taken before 30 June, but cannot be taken during Christmas, New Year or Easter holidays.

When you have named all the animals, complete the following sentence, in not more than 15 words.

I would like to join the safari in Phinda because ....
....

Read these statements about different parts of the text. They are all false.
Can you say why? Complete the explanations of what makes the statements wrong.

a If you name all the animals, you will win a prize.
False, because you must not only name the animals, you must also _____

b You can see the mountains from the campsite.
False. It is not the campsite which has a view of the mountains, but _____

c CCA has introduced new kinds of wildlife to Phinda.
Untrue, because the kinds of wildlife which have come into Phinda are not _____

d You'll see rhinos on your morning walk.
False. 'You'll see rhinos' is much stronger than '_____ to spot rhinos' in the text.

e Dinner will be served for you in your tent.
False. We don't know where dinner will be _____ , only where it will be _____

f You'll have to wash your own clothes while on safari.
Not true. The text says that the holiday includes _____

g Winners can claim their prize at any time.
Wrong. The last sentence in the text says that winners must take their prize _____;
they can't take their prize _____

→ **See page 93 for Supplementary Activities. More True or false practice in Unit 6.**

Reading

In the exam

In Part 3 of the Reading Test, you will read one long text, and answer ten true or false questions.

In this unit

- Making 'true' statements
- Being the examiner
- Exam practice for Part 3

To start you thinking … about feeling good and feeling bad

1 🎧 Listen to this poem (you can read it on page 134). Think about the person who is speaking. What kind of life does he have? What kind of work does he do? Where does he live?

A lot of things made this a bad day for the man. Find four of them.

In pairs, talk together about what makes a bad day for you. What do you do if you have a bad day? Use these ideas or some of your own.

do some sport	listen to music	have a bath
eat some chocolate	text a friend	kick the cat
turn off your mobile	buy something new	go for a walk

Making 'true' statements

2 In Unit 5, you looked at why statements are *false*. Now the focus is on what makes them *true*.

Read the information about chocolate.

Would you like some chocolate?

a It's many people's favourite food – and if the latest evidence is to be believed, the last thing you should feel when you secretly enjoy a bar of chocolate is guilty. Last week scientists revealed that eating chocolate makes you feel emotionally better and so the smooth running of your body is improved.

b Researchers at Harvard University in the US studied 8,000 men for 65 years and found that those who ate small amounts of chocolate up to three times a month, lived almost a year longer than those who didn't eat any. They concluded that this is because cocoa (which is the main ingredient of chocolate) contains something which fights cholesterol.

c If you're feeling that everything is too much for you, have a bit of chocolate. Chocolate contains sugar, which we think is bad for us, but it has been shown to have a calming and pain-relieving effect on people and animals. Also the smell of chocolate slows down our brain waves, which again makes us feel calm.

d Although many teenagers blame chocolate for the spots on their faces, there's no scientific data for this. In a scientific experiment, a group of teenagers were given chocolate to eat, and it was found that their skin didn't change.

e Most people do believe, however, that eating chocolate makes you fat. Well, you can't blame any single food for an increase in your weight. Just remember, if you burn off more calories than you eat, you'll be fine.

f Do you find that the middle of the afternoon is a low time for your brain? That's the time when your blood sugar levels are getting a bit low. Try eating chocolate in the middle of the afternoon, you'll find that your mind is more focused.

Look at these incomplete statements about the text (there is one statement for each paragraph). Fill the gaps in order to make each statement *true*.

a You don't need to _____ _____ when you eat chocolate.
b Chocolate can make you _____ _____ .
c Chocolate is _____ _____ stress.
d Chocolate _____ _____ you spots.
e Chocolate alone doesn't make you _____ _____ weight.
f Chocolate can help you _____ better.

Being the examiner

3 If you're feeling really fed up and chocolate doesn't help, how about some exercise? Read this text.

The Ups and Downs of 50 Years of Running

1951

The first jogger was a fat New Zealander who wanted to get into shape. He worked in a shoe factory and played rugby at the weekends but couldn't lose any weight. He knew he couldn't run fast like everyone else was trying to do at that time, so he decided to run slowly for long distances. His weight went down and he developed a passion for running. Eventually, he represented his country in an international competition.

1972

The marathon runner Frank Shorter won the gold medal for the USA at the Munich Olympics. As a result, a running boom hit the States – everyone started running through the streets of the cities, including the president at that time, Jimmy Carter. The world watched him on their TVs as he collapsed by the side of the road. This public exhibition didn't stop him – he is still running!

1981

At the first ever London Marathon, there were two winners of the men's race. They decided to cross the finishing line together. Behind them were 6,253 runners. The following year, 90,000 people applied to run the course.

1987

A 42-year old British woman who had stopped smoking and started training only a year before, set a new record time in the London Marathon. She then went on to win the New York marathon as well. Millions of people cheered her achievements, but then realised that there was no excuse anymore – if she could do it, so could they!

2002

A record 32,000 people finished the 2002 London Marathon. In the last 20 years, the race has raised over £100m for many different charities.

Student A: Complete the statements below, according to the instructions.
Student B: Turn to page 102. Complete the statements according to the instructions.

Student A

Complete these four statements on *The Ups and Downs of 50 Years of Running*, using the words below. If you see **F**, make the statement false. If you see **T**, make the statement true.

two   smoking   lost   running   died   agreement

a The New Zealander _____ weight by _____ quickly. **F**
b The US President _____ while running in a race. **F**
c In the 1981 London Marathon, the _____ winners had an _____ that they would finish together. **T**
d The winner of the London Marathon in 1987 gave up _____ a few years before. **F**

Write these four complete statements (without **T/F**) on a piece of paper. Give it to your partner to decide if the statements are *true* or *false*.

➜ **See page 93 for Supplementary Activities. See page 22 for Exam practice for Part 3.**

Exam practice for Part 3

Exam tip

- The statements are in the same order as the information given in the text.
- When you practise, try different ways of reading and see which is better for you.
  Method 1: Read one or two statements, then read the first part of the text.
  Method 2: Read the first part of the text, then the first two statements.

Look at the sentences below about choosing a gym.
Read the text on the opposite page to decide if each sentence is correct (T) or incorrect (F).
If it is correct, circle T.
If it is not correct, circle F.

1 Money is not the only thing to think about before joining a gym.	T F
2 A good gym will expect you to join for a full year.	T F
3 If you stop using the gym for any reason, you'll have to give up your membership.	T F
4 The total number of members is less important than the number who regularly use the gym.	T F
5 Lots of equipment means it's a good gym to join.	T F
6 Monday evening is the worst time to see a gym.	T F
7 If the staff are happy, they don't need qualifications.	T F
8 It's a good idea to check the gym has enough members of staff.	T F
9 You can tell how good a gym is by what happens on your first visit.	T F
10 Talking to a current member can be helpful.	T F

Choosing a gym

How much does it cost?

Find out exactly what the membership includes. Be careful, because some gyms charge a joining fee as well as the membership fee. When you know how much you have to pay, ask yourself, "Am I going to find the time to come to the gym regularly?" If the answer is "Yes", then read on ….

Try it first

It may be possible to get a free trial – perhaps a couple of visits in order to get the 'feel' of a gym, and see if it's really suitable for you. Some gyms offer a two or three month membership for first-timers – they hope that people will like the gym enough to want to continue, and next time will pay for an annual membership.

What if there's a problem?

Sometimes, something like an injury or illness or a job move means you can't use your gym membership. A good club will be sympathetic and should, at the very least, allow you to freeze your membership and then use it again when you're ready, or give you back your money.

Who are the members?

Try and find out how many active members the gym has. If a club has 10,000 members but only 1,000 are active ones, it doesn't give you very much confidence. A club with 2,000 members and 700 active ones shows that its members must be happy and satisfied with the service they are getting.

What about the equipment?

You walk in and see 40–50 pieces of equipment and you think "That's great – I'll never have to queue for equipment". But remember, some clubs have really big memberships. Surprisingly, Monday evenings between 6.00 and 8.00 are the busiest time of the week, so this is a good time to go along and check out the worst possible situation!

And the staff?

It's the instructors and trainers that make a great gym. Some gyms try to attract members through their luxury facilities and high-tech equipment. So don't just think what an amazing swimming pool, check that the staff are qualified for their jobs. Do they seem happy in their work? Are there enough of them around at busy times? Do they look interested in the members or are they more interested in showing off their own bodies?

Are you welcome?

Many gyms do wonderful things for new members on their first visit, for example one-to-one instruction with a personal fitness programme, as well as perhaps advice on eating and diets. But in many cases, that's it. It seems that when you've given them your money for the year, they suddenly lose interest in you. The best thing you can do is find someone who has already joined the gym and ask them what their experiences are of the service that is offered.

Reading

In the exam

In Part 4 of the Reading Test, you will read a text and answer five multiple-choice questions. The text will often express feelings, opinions and attitudes.

In this unit

- Understanding feelings
- What's the writer trying to do?

To start you thinking ... about your experiences

1 **In pairs, discuss your answers to these questions.**

1 What makes you angry? Why?
2 What song or piece of music is your favourite at the moment? Why?
3 How good are you at doing jobs in the house?

4 Who was the first person you spoke to when you got up this morning?
5 What keeps you awake at nights?
6 What makes life fun at the moment?

Understanding feelings

2 **This man answered some of the questions in exercise 1.**
   Read what he says. Which question (1–6 above) does each answer match?

a My wife, Catherine. She's great in the mornings. Normally I like to get up early too. At the moment though, I don't really see mornings – I mean I'm in a show at the local theatre which finishes about 11 o'clock and then I need at least a couple of hours to relax – I hate going to bed, but I'm a good sleeper when I do make it.

Matches question: ...

b Well, I don't cook. When I'm hungry I just want to eat – the idea of planning a meal is not something I'm good at. I do a bit of vacuuming now and again and I'm capable of cleaning the bath – I wish I had more time to do ironing because I find that really calming.

Matches question: ...

c My daughter and my dog – and probably both for the same reason – they're full of energy and every day is full of new opportunities. Just seeing them makes me smile.

Matches question: ...

d Well, the world is not exactly a happy place, is it? Watching the news on TV late at night is not good for my state of mind, but as I said generally I sleep well. If I have real problems getting to sleep, I just read for a bit.

Matches question: ...

3 **Look again at the man's answers, and find what his feelings, opinions and attitudes are about certain things.**
   a What two things make him happy? _his daughter and_ _____ (paragraph c)
   b What's he good at? _____ (paragraph a)
   c What's he unhappy about? _____ (paragraph d)
   d What's he not good at? _____ (paragraph b)
   e What does he think about housework? _____ (paragraph b)

4 Now answer these multiple-choice questions: there is only one correct answer.

a What are the man's sleeping habits like?
  A He wakes up earlier than he would like to.
  B He hates having too little sleep.
  C He likes to go to bed early when he can.
  D He has no problems at all with his sleep.

b What are the man's feelings about housework?
  A It's not very important in his life.
  B He loves doing it when he has to.
  C He leaves it all for other people to do.
  D It takes too much time in his life.

c What do you learn about this person from his answers?
  A He is unemployed.
  B He has a lot of spare time.
  C He is an actor.
  D He is a TV performer.

What's the writer trying to do?

5 Some of the multiple-choice questions in this part of the exam might ask about why the writer has written the text and what you, the reader, learn from it.

Read part of a magazine article by Maisie McNeice, who is co-author of a book about her childhood in Africa.

When I was seven, my family moved to Botswana, because my mother wanted us to experience a different way of life. We joined an international group of scientists at a lion research station, and for five years now we've been living in tents in the middle of nowhere. In my book, there are lots of funny stories about our lives here. For example, when I go to bed, I have to check for scorpions before I get in – but I don't mind that. The only thing I regret is not having walls to put posters on. There's a kitchen tent and a living room tent with a video, so I can still watch *Friends* in the evenings.

There are no fences around our camp, and it's dangerous to walk around after dark, so we drive – even from the lounge tent to my bedroom tent! Occasionally I think "What if an animal is lying round the corner and kills me!" but usually I'm fine. Once I turned a corner in the car (I've driven since I was nine) and there was a huge bull elephant, and I stalled the car. Luckily the elephant swerved and missed us, but not by much! Another time my brother trod on a scorpion, and he was in agony for days. And we get spiders in our tents, the size of CDs, but I'm not scared of them. And as for lions, I started working with them when I was nine, and they're just the most wonderful creatures in the world.

Put these sentences in the order that the information comes in the text.

Maisie …
a admits she sometimes feels afraid. ....
b tells us something she'd like. ....
c describes a dangerous situation she was once in. ....
d describes the research station's facilities. ....
e says why her family moved to Africa. 1
f explains what she does before going to bed. ....
g describes her feelings about lions. ....

6 Now answer these multiple-choice questions. After you've chosen an answer, circle the letter at the end of the line. If your choices are correct, these letters will spell a word from the text.

1 What is Maisie's main reason for writing in the magazine?
  A She wants to interest people in her book. **T**
  B She hopes to save lions from being killed. **L**
  C She must do it as part of her job. **F**
  D She was asked to do it by her family. **M**

2 Why did Maisie's family move to Botswana?
  A To do some research into lions. **H**
  B Because they enjoyed living in tents. **I**
  C Because it's such a beautiful country. **O**
  D To have a new kind of lifestyle. **E**

3 The creature which put Maisie in most danger was
  A an elephant **N**
  B a scorpion **W**
  C a spider **E**
  D a lion **O**

4 What does Maisie feel about spiders?
  A They are not dangerous. **N**
  B They don't frighten her. **T**
  C Her brother shouldn't worry about them. **S**
  D People should not let them come into their tents. **R**

5 What would be a good title for Maisie's book?
  A Life with the Lions **S**
  B African Life **E**
  C Travels around Africa **N**
  D My unusual family **M**

→ See page 93 for Supplementary Activities.
More multiple-choice practice in Unit 8.

Reading

In the exam

In Part 4 of the Reading Test, you will read a text and answer five multiple-choice questions. The text will often express feelings, opinions and attitudes.

In this unit

- Sharing information
- Answering multiple-choice questions
- Exam practice for Part 4

To start you thinking ... about when you were 12

1 In two minutes, write down six things you remember about your life when you were 12. In pairs, compare your lists.

Sharing information

2 This exercise gives you practice in understanding people's feelings and attitudes. You are going to read what Kate and Debbie remember about their lives when they were 12.
Student B: Turn to page 102 for Debbie's story.
Student A: Read Kate's story and make notes on what she says about:

a clothes: _No money for new clothes;_   b school: _____

c girl/boy relationships: _____   d housework: _____

Now answer the following multiple-choice questions. Write your answers on a separate piece of paper.

e What is Kate's main point about clothes?
  A They never had any new ones.
  B They had to make their own.
  C They thought they were very unattractive.
  D They had to look after the clothes that they had.

f What does Kate say about her school?
  A It was not as good as many of today's schools.
  B It was out in the country.
  C The teachers were stricter with the boys than with the girls.
  D She could play with her friend, Dorothy, there.

g What do we learn about relationships between boys and girls?
  A They were only able to meet at school.
  B They had quite a natural relationship.
  C They hardly ever met each other.
  D They could only meet when on holiday.

h What does Kate say about housework?
  A She doesn't mention it at all.
  B She remembers finding it very tiring after a day at school.
  C She says it stopped her from doing other things.
  D She thinks that she quite enjoyed it.

Kate's story

When I was 12 ... in 1912

We were not rich. New clothes were rare, if you tore something you had to mend it. Our dresses were plain and we had to wear aprons over them to keep them clean. We also wore plenty of underwear to keep warm as there was no heating. I can remember not liking the winter very much!

I have a very strong memory of seeing a car for the first time. We couldn't believe our eyes – I was used to horses, you see. We lived in the country so I had to walk about 2 kms to school every day. The teachers were strict and girls and boys were taught separately. I think it's much better now when they're both taught together – more natural isn't it? My mother told me not to talk to the boys but never explained why. I didn't know anything about sex until, aged 15, a nurse showed me some diagrams – I was so shocked I fainted!

I wasn't allowed to go out much because I always had to help my mother in the house. I only saw my friend, Dorothy, at school but we got to play together a bit in the summer holidays when we went to the beach near our village. That was the best bit.

When you're ready, ask your partner what Debbie said about the four topics, a–d.

When you've received all the information from your partner:

Student A: Turn to page 102 and answer the multiple-choice questions on Debbie's story.
Student B: Look at page 26 and answer the multiple-choice questions on Kate's story.
When you've both finished, check that you have the same answers.

Answering multiple-choice questions

3 Kate and Debbie's stories were part of a TV programme called *When we were 12.*
Read this review of the programme by a TV critic.

Bret Chrysler's latest idea for a TV documentary (*When we were 12* Monday 8.00 pm) was, I'm sure, a result of the huge success he'd had with *Now we are 80* last year. That was fresh and full of humour and the extraordinary men and women he found to tell their stories were a delight to listen to. Chrysler didn't find it necessary to add anything to them. But with *When we were 12*, half the programme was taken up with old news films from the times, or computer imagery of, for example, the sinking of the *Titanic*. What the point of that was I'll never know. Too many directors nowadays seem to think that viewers will get bored watching people talking to the camera, telling their story. They feel the need to show some action. Well, I for one don't agree. Give me a good actor and/or a good story and I'm happy.

The stories and memories from last night's programme were a mixture of the ordinary and the unusual. What was good was that you could learn a lot – what the normal behaviour was at the time, how much an ice cream cost in 1930, what the attitude was to the opposite sex. It was in many ways a fascinating programme of social history. But then, just as I was enjoying the trip down memory lane, one of those irritating bits of news film interrupted.

In 1–4 below, think of your answer *before* you look at the A, B, C, D choices.

1 What's the writer trying to do in the text?
   A give her opinion of the director
   B compare this programme with an earlier one
   C explain why the programme was made
   D describe some ways in which the programme failed

2 How did the writer feel about *Now we are 80?*
   A She thought something needed adding to it.
   B She thought it was an excellent programme.
   C She didn't like the old films that were in it.
   D She felt it needed more action.

3 What does the reader learn about the writer from the text?
   A She doesn't get bored watching people telling their own stories.
   B She doesn't like any of Bret Chrysler's work.
   C She dislikes news films being shown on TV.
   D She doesn't enjoy TV documentaries.

4 What did the writer enjoy about *When we were 12*?
   A The details of everyday life
   B The action in many of the scenes
   C The use of modern technology
   D The good acting

You may have to look at different parts of the text to find all the information for this last question.

5 Which one of these summaries in a TV guide best describes *When we were 12*?
   A This programme brings together real people who, now in their 80s, look back at their lives when they were 12 years old.
   B This programme looks at the world through the eyes of 12-year-old children from all over the world. It'll make you laugh and cry.
   C Everyone will enjoy this entertaining and informative programme in which real people remember how the world was at different times during the last century.
   D A 12-year-old child gives a personal view of her life in the last century. The programme includes some amazing film of the *Titanic's* last moments.

➔ See page 94 for Supplementary Activities.
See page 28 for Exam practice for Part 4.

Exam practice for Part 4

Exam tip

- Read the text twice so you understand it well.
- Try to answer the questions yourself before you look at the **A, B, C, D** choices.
- If you're not sure of the right answer, cross out the answers you know are wrong.

Read the text and questions.
For each question, choose the correct answer A, B, C or D.

Letter to editor of TV Weekly

Dear Sir/Madam

I read Alison Burnham's review of *When we were 12*, and I do not agree with her. I thought the programme was wonderful – I found the old news pictures really interesting – they helped to bring to life the stories the people were telling.

After watching the programme, I kept remembering things from my own childhood. For example, one day when I was about five, I was going to school on the bus by myself (this was the late 1940s). My mother had given me exactly the right money for a return ticket. I held out my hand with the money in it – one big coin on top of one little coin. The bus conductor took the big top coin only and she gave me a ticket, but it was a pink one for a single journey. I needed a white one for a return journey, but I was too frightened to say anything. When school finished for the day, I couldn't catch the bus home – I had to walk. As an adult, whenever I've been in a situation where I need to say something or take some action, this early memory of my bus ride comes back to me, and I'm able to take control of the situation.

I would like to say to the director, Bret Chrysler, carry on making this kind of programme. Too much TV these days is quiz shows and so-called 'reality programmes'. I appreciate the human story that can make me laugh and cry.

Yours faithfully
Chris Daniels

1 What is Chris Daniels' reason for sending this letter?
   A He thinks Alison will be interested in his childhood story.
   B He wants to describe his feelings about the programme.
   C He wants Alison to change her opinion.
   D He hopes that other readers will support him.

2 Chris Daniels includes the story about the bus ticket
   A because it's similar to one of the stories on the TV programme.
   B to show how the programme made him think.
   C because he thinks the readers of TV Weekly will enjoy it.
   D to talk about how miserable his childhood was.

3 In the story about the bus ticket, why did Chris Daniels have to walk home?
   A The bus was late.
   B The conductor didn't want him on the bus.
   C He hadn't got a return ticket.
   D He had lost his bus ticket.

4 What does Chris Daniels now think about his experience on the bus?
   A He believes it helps him to be more confident.
   B He wishes it hadn't happened.
   C He remembers it every time he gets on a bus.
   D He feels angry when he thinks about it.

5 Which of these sentences would Chris Daniels be most pleased to read in a reply
   to his letter?
   A You'll be interested to know that we've received letters both 'for' and 'against'
   this programme.
   B We are pleased to tell you that the TV company has promised to show fewer old
   news pictures.
   C We're always happy to know what our readers think about TV programmes.
   D You'll be pleased to know that the TV company has just told us that work will
   start on a second series in the autumn.

Reading

UNIT 9 Multiple-choice gap fill (1)

In the exam

In Part 5 of the Reading Test you will read a short text with ten 'gaps' in it. You fill the gap by choosing from four multiple-choice options.

In this unit

- Practice with key grammar
- Practice with key vocabulary
- Thinking about grammar and meaning

To start you thinking … about houses and homes

1 Look at the following groups of words. They're all connected with houses.
  In pairs, you have two minutes to decide which word is the odd one out in each group, and why.

  a pillow   (towel)   duvet   sheet *(all others are found on a bed)*
  b sitting room   lounge   attic   living room
  c garden   fence   balcony   gate
  d tent   cottage   villa   apartment
  e cooker   sink   freezer   fridge
  f ceiling   floor   shelf   wall

Practice with key grammar

2 In the exam, some of the gaps in the text will test grammatical structures.
  The structures include 'quantity' words (e.g. *several, some, no, many*).

  'Quantity' words
  Look at this description of someone's bedroom. Choose two correct 'quantity' expressions for each sentence (see Grammar File, page 111).

  In the bedroom
  - there's some electronic equipment with a **(1) lot / few / many / number** of wires in the corner of the room.
  - there are posters on **(2) any / all / every / each** wall.
  - there are **(3) several / couple / some / plenty** dirty coffee cups on the desk.
  - there are **(4) some / many / lots / plenty** of CDs beside the bed for people to borrow.
  - there isn't **(5) much / more / some / enough** room to sit down.

3 Imagine you're designing your own perfect room. Think of six things you would put in it and where, and tell your partner. Use the language below.

I'd like I'd have There'd be	lots of some a few every	on beside between in in front of

  e.g. I'd like a few plants on the floor of my room.

30

Practice with key vocabulary

4 This part of the exam also tests your vocabulary. The pairs of words in the exercise below have *similar* meanings but not *exactly* the same. Choose the correct word for each sentence.

The house of the future

a You'll never again have to .... to turn the lights off when you go out – the central computer will do it automatically.
remember   **remind**

b I'd like a 'smart' fridge that can .... me when I need to buy more milk, for example.
say   **tell**

c Robots that can .... the ironing would be a good idea for the future.
make   **do**

d If people come to visit you when you're out, they can .... a video message on the panel at the front door.
let   **leave**

e It will be impossible for thieves to .... a house because of the security systems.
rob   **steal**

f People will do all their work from home, so business .... will become less necessary.
travels   **trips**

g If you'd like a beautiful .... from your house, just press a button and choose between 'virtual' mountains, the ocean or a city.
view   **scenery**

Thinking about grammar and meaning

5 The word you choose to fill the gap in Part 5
• must 'fit' grammatically
• must 'fit' with the meaning of the sentence

Read the text. Then fill each gap with *one* suitable word of your own. Use the 'clues' to help you. (Don't look at the A, B, C, D choices yet.) Think carefully about the *meaning* of what you're reading.

An unusual place to live

Joanne Ussery lives on a plane. **(0)** _In/During_ the mid-1990s, this Boeing 727 was still **(1)** .... regularly **(2)** .... Florida and the Caribbean. Now it **(3)** .... be one of the most unusual homes in the world. She **(4)** .... the 27-year-old plane for about $3,000. Then it was moved to the plot of land that she owns. At first, she had a **(5)** .... problems because people came and **(6)** .... parts of the plane. But since she has been living there, it has been fine. She has tried to use **(7)** .... part of the plane – the bathroom is in the cockpit **(8)** .... the pilots used to sit, then there are three bedrooms, and a long sitting room, complete with four emergency exit doors which can be opened on summer evenings to **(9)** .... in some fresh air. The kitchen is at the back of the plane. Joanne's only problem now is the **(10)** .... of 'tourists' who turn up, wanting to look around her home.

Clues
0 preposition of time
1 verb, in continuous form – what do planes do?
2 preposition of place/movement – two places are mentioned
3 modal auxiliary verb
4 verb, past tense – read to the end of the sentence
5 'quantity' word – how many problems?
6 verb, past tense – what might people do that would cause a problem?
7 'quantity' word – be careful, it's followed by a singular noun 'part'
8 relative pronoun; it relates back to 'the cockpit'
9 verb, infinitive form – by opening the doors you allow the air to come in
10 noun

Now, compare your answers with the A, B, C, D choices. Choose the correct one.

0 A At   (B) In   C On   D For
1 A driving   B sailing   C flying   D moving
2 A among   B by   C into   D between
3 A should   B ought   C would   D must
4 A paid   B bought   C spent   D charged
5 A lot   B couple   C many   D few
6 A robbed   B kept   C stole   D brought
7 A every   B all   C several   D one
8 A that   B which   C where   D there
9 A offer   B give   C change   D let
10 A amount   B size   C total   D number

→ **See page 94 for Supplementary Activities.**

Reading

In the exam

In Part 5 of the Reading Test you will read a short text with ten 'gaps' in it. You fill the gap by choosing from four multiple-choice options.

In this unit

- Practice with key grammar
- Practice with key vocabulary
- Exam practice for Part 5

To start you thinking … about money

1 In pairs, you have two minutes to write down as many verbs as you can connected with money.

e.g. to earn

You might find some of your 'money' verbs in the next text.

Practice with key grammar

2 **Prepositions**

Some gaps in the text in Part 5 will test prepositions. Often a preposition goes together with the word **before** it (e.g. interested *in*), or **after** it (e.g. *by* mistake).
Read the text. Look carefully at the words before and after each gap.
Fill each gap with a preposition. Use the prepositions in the box below (see Appendix 2, page 117).

Spend or save?

Imagine you had 10,000 euros to invest, what would you do with it? How do you know which companies would be good ones for your money? Should you ask (0) ..for.. help from a professional person or can you decide (1) .... your own?
The Economics Department of a British university set up an experiment to see if it's worth paying (2) .... professional financial advice. A successful financial adviser and a child of five were both given 10,000 euros to invest in four different companies.

The financial adviser, Mark Lytton, believed he was very good (3) .... his job and chose his companies very carefully. Five-year-old Mia Beech picked her four companies (4) .... 100 pieces of paper thrown off a balcony.
(5) .... the end of the first year, Mia had earned 5.8% (about 580 euros) and the financial adviser had lost 46%. In order to continue the experiment, Mark Lytton needed to borrow money (6) .... Mia. What does this prove? That it's better to depend (7) .... luck than professional advice, or maybe we should forget about trying to make money – just spend it all (8) .... something we really want.

| at | on | from | from | ~~for~~ | on | on | for | at |

There were seven different verbs connected with money in the text. Can you find them?

3 Linking words

Here's another way to lose your money quickly.

Read the text. Circle the correct 'linking' word. Only *one* is correct each time.

(see Grammar File, page 108)

The Chicken Challenge

Chickens are lovely animals **(0) and / so /** but nobody thinks of them as being intelligent. At a casino in Indiana, USA, customers were offered $5,000 to beat a chicken at the game of noughts and crosses. Soon there were queues of people waiting to play **(1) until / because / however** they thought it would be easy to win money.

The chicken stands in a glass cage **(2) or / and / but** pecks its moves with its beak, on a touch-sensitive panel on the glass. The first surprise that the customers get comes **(3) while / before / when** they discover that the chicken has been 'taught' what to do, and **(4) since / then / until** they find out that the chicken always gets the first move in the game. People who have played noughts and crosses will know that it's very hard to win **(5) because / if / unless** you're the one who makes the first move. In fact, **(6) when / from / since** the Chicken Challenge started, only five humans have won. People still believe they can beat the chicken **(7) although / but / so** they keep on trying, which makes the casino owners very happy. It's not clear if the chicken **(8) or / and / nor** the customers get more pleasure from the experience.

Practice with key vocabulary

4 The gaps in this text focus on vocabulary. Look at the three choices given; they are all *wrong*. Write the *correct* word in D (sometimes there is more than one possible answer).

The Californian Gold Rush

In 1848, gold was **(0)** .... in California. When the **(1)** .... of this was made public, tens of thousands of hopeful people set out for the golden land. They dreamt of **(2)** .... rich but their experiences were very different.

Many died on the journey but by 1849, 80,000 people had **(3)** .... in California. They spread out through the mountain valleys and began **(4)** .... for the gold. Gold towns, for example San Francisco, **(5)** .... from tiny villages to busy towns almost overnight. Most men **(6)** .... very little money, and the **(7)** .... of food was high. The towns were violent **(8)** .... and fights happened every day; for the few women who lived there, the **(9)** .... of life must have been terrible.

There have been other examples of 'gold fever' in history, but American cowboy films have made the Great Californian Gold Rush the most **(10)** .... one.

	A		B		C		D
0	A explored		B invented		C made		D *found/discovered*
1	A information		B notice		C announcement		D
2	A finding		B making		C earning		D
3	A reached		B come		C gone		D
4	A noticing		B watching		C seeing		D
5	A became		B got		C appeared		D
6	A won		B bought		C paid		D
7	A charge		B amount		C quality		D
8	A positions		B parts		C spaces		D
9	A habit		B custom		C manner		D
10	A known		B noticed		C public		D

→ See page 94 for Supplementary Activities.
See page 34 for Exam practice for Part 5.

Exam practice for Part 5

Exam tip

- It's important to understand what the text is about, so try and read it once without looking at the choices.
- Read the words before and after the gap very carefully so that your choice makes sense grammatically.
- Check that the word you choose makes sense in the sentence.

Read the text below and choose the correct word for each space.
Circle the correct letter A, B, C or D.

WHO WANTS TO BE A MILLIONAIRE?

The world's most (0) ..C.. TV quiz show started in the UK in 1998. The idea has now spread to over 100 countries, including Greece and Spain.

One person, the contestant, must answer 15 multiple-choice questions correctly to win the £1m top (1) .... If at any (2) .... they answer incorrectly, the game is over. A computer selects the questions from a database of 2,500. (3) .... that point, nobody knows (4) .... questions are about to be asked.

The programme gets more (5) .... as the money increases. Now contestants are really afraid (6) .... making a mistake. It's possible, (7) .... unusual, for a contestant to leave the show with (8) .... money at all.
Contestants can get help. One way is to "Phone a friend". They may speak to a friend (9) .... the phone for 30 seconds to (10) .... the question.

The phrase "Can I phone a friend?" has now become part of modern everyday English.
You use it when you want to say "I don't know the answer".

0 **A** regular   **B** typical   **Ⓒ** popular   **D** basic

1 **A** award   **B** amount   **C** winning   **D** prize

2 **A** time   **B** day   **C** period   **D** hour

3 **A** From   **B** Until   **C** Since   **D** On

4 **A** what   **B** the   **C** that   **D** some

5 **A** strong   **B** important   **C** serious   **D** firm

6 **A** to   **B** of   **C** for   **D** by

7 **A** or   **B** even   **C** and   **D** but

8 **A** no   **B** some   **C** any   **D** much

9 **A** by   **B** with   **C** on   **D** in

10 **A** talk   **B** chat   **C** argue   **D** discuss

Writing

UNIT 1 Sentence transformation (1)

In the exam

In Part 1 of the Writing Test you will 'transform' five sentences by rewriting them with different words that give the same meaning. The beginning and end of each sentence is given. You must write no more than three words. This part tests your grammar.

In this unit

- Saying things another way
- Matching the meaning
- Practice with key grammar
  - present perfect/past tense
  - 'negative/positive' expressions
  - passive/active forms

To start you thinking ... about holidays

1 In pairs, ask and answer. Make complete questions.

- When / last holiday? Where / go?
- any plans / this year?
- Where / like to go / if / had / chance?

Saying things another way

2 Monika is on holiday in Mexico. She's meeting some other guests at her hotel.

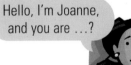

Hello, I'm Joanne, and you are ...?

I'm Monika.

Someone else asked her the same thing, but used different words:

Hi, my name's Arnie. What's your name?

My name's Monika.

Read the postcard that Monika has written to her English friend, Sue. She wants to say the same things but in a different way to another friend, Anna. Using the words that are given, write her postcard to Anna.

Hi Sue
I'm having a wonderful time here in Acapulco.
The weather's been great.
Only one day of rain!
It's a very interesting city.
The hotel has a great swimming pool.
Hope you've remembered I'll be in Oxford next week.
Give your brother my love.
Monika

Sue Cox
14 Whitelands Rd
Oxford
OX40 3KU

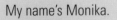

Hi Anna
a I'm _really enjoying myself_ in Acapulco.
b It's _____ weather.
c It's _____ rained _____ .
d The city _____ .
e There _____ the hotel.
f Hope _____ forgotten I'll be in Oxford next week.
g _____ to your brother.
Monika

Matching the meaning

3 In this part of the exam, you're given a sentence and you must complete a *similar* sentence using different words that give the same meaning. Find a connection between a phrase from **A** and a phrase from **B**.

A	B
everybody hates	belong to
not allowed	Why don't you
whose	nobody likes
If I were you	can't
how much	Let's
name	cost
What about	is called

Use a phrase from A or B to rewrite each sentence so that it means the same as the first.

a **If I were you**, I'd put a hat on – the sun's very strong.
Why _don't you put a hat on_ ?

b What's that famous Aztec city **called**?
What's .... that famous Aztec city?

c What's the **cost** of the trip?
How .... ?

d **Whose** camera is this?
Who does .... ?

e You **can't** smoke on the coach.
You're ....

f **Everybody hates** long coach journeys.
.... likes long coach journeys.

g **What about** going for a swim after we get back from our visit?
.... a swim after we get back from our visit.

Practice with key grammar

4 This part of the exam will test a variety of grammar structures. In this exercise, you will practise rewriting sentences which include
- present perfect or past tense   a–d
- 'negative/positive' expressions   e–f
- active or passive forms   g–h
(See Grammar File, pages 105, 106 and 111)

Monika's parents are planning their holiday in India. Look at these sentences and the words on the right. Circle the correct one.

The Taj Mahal, Agra

a The last time Monika's parents had a holiday was three years ago.
Monika's parents haven't had a holiday .... three years.

(for)/ since

b They haven't been abroad for a long time.
It's a long time .... they've been abroad.

since/that

c They've never travelled outside Europe before.
This will be the first time they .... outside Europe.

travelled/have travelled

d They're still thinking about what to take with them to India.
They still .... what to take with them to India.

didn't decide/haven't decided

e There aren't many cheap flights from Europe to India.
There are only .... cheap flights from Europe to India.

some/a few

f The Taj Mahal is in Agra, which is quite near the capital of India.
Agra is not .... the capital of India.

far to/far from

g The Taj Mahal was built by Emperor Shah Jahan.
Emperor Shah Jahan .... the Taj Mahal.

build/built

h The Taj Mahal is visited by millions of tourists every year.
Millions of tourists .... the Taj Mahal every year.

are visiting/visit

Here are some sentences about the hotel where Monika's parents are going to stay. For each question, complete the second sentence so that it means the same as the first, *using no more than three words.*

i The hotel became part of the Hilton International Group six weeks ago.
The hotel .... part of the Hilton International Group for six weeks.

j There aren't many guests at the hotel yet.
The hotel .... only a few guests at the moment.

k The furniture in the rooms was chosen by India's top designer.
India's top designer .... in the rooms.

l The hotel is not far from the Taj Mahal.
The Taj Mahal is quite .... the hotel.

What do *you* think about going on holiday with your family? What's good or bad about it? You have three minutes to think of as many ideas as possible. Compare them with a partner.

→ See page 95 for Supplementary Activities. More sentence transformation practice in Unit 2.

Writing

UNIT 2 Sentence transformation (2)

In the exam

In Part 1 of the Writing Test you will 'transform' five sentences by rewriting them with different words that give the same meaning. The beginning and end of each sentence is given. You must write no more than three words. This part tests your grammar.

In this unit

- Same message, different words
- Practice with key grammar
  - comparison
  - indirect/direct speech
- Changing between verbs and nouns

To start you thinking … about how people look

1 **In pairs, talk about these sentences.**

   a Small tattoos are quite popular with a lot of teenagers.
   b I was forbidden to colour my hair when I was younger.
   c Only a few people I know have pierced noses.
   d It's ages since I changed my hairstyle.
   e I never let anyone borrow my clothes.
   f Hair gel is very popular.
   g No-one in my class has red hair.
   h Most people prefer trainers to ordinary shoes.
   i I never wear sunglasses, except after a late night.

Same message, different words

2 **Look again at the sentences a–i above. Each one can be expressed in a different way. Complete each of the sentences below to give the same meaning. You can use as many words as you like, but you must include the word(s) in bold.**

   a A lot of teenagers _like small tattoos_ .   **like**
   b I .... when I was younger.   **allowed**
   c .... have pierced noses.   **Not many**
   d I .... ages.   **haven't**
   e I never .... anyone.   **lend**
   f .... hair gel.   **Everyone**
   g .... with red hair.   **There**
   h Most people .... ordinary shoes.   **think … better**
   i I .... after a late night.   **only**

38

Practice with key grammar

3 In this exercise you will practise rewriting sentences which use
* different ways of comparing   a–f
* indirect speech   g–i
(see Grammar File, pages 109 and 112)

Rosa is describing her family. Look at the sentences and the choice of words on the right. Circle the correct word(s).

a My sister, Adriana, has longer hair than me.
My hair is not as long .... Adriana's.   **than / as**

b She buys more clothes than I do.
I .... as many clothes as she does.   **don't buy / buy**

c My four-year-old brother Marco prefers computer games to clothes.
My brother Marco likes computer games .... clothes.   **as well as / more than**

d Mum says Marco is too young to choose his own clothes.
Mum says Marco isn't .... to choose his own clothes.   **old enough / enough old**

e During the week, my older brother Gino doesn't have enough time to think about his appearance.
During the week, Gino is .... to think about his appearance.   **too busy / very busy**

f But on Saturdays, he's better dressed than any other man in town.
On Saturdays, Gino is .... dressed man in town.   **the better / the best**

g Adriana asked me why I wanted to borrow her clothes.
"Why .... to borrow my clothes?" asked Adriana.   **did you want / do you want**

h Adriana told me not to get them dirty.
Adriana said, "Rosa, please .... them dirty."   **to not get / don't get**

i Mum asked me why I was wearing Adriana's clothes.
Mum asked, "Why .... Adriana's clothes?"   **you are wearing / are you wearing**

Changing between verbs and nouns

4 Sometimes you need to change the form of a word e.g. from a verb to a noun.

to choose	to compare	to argue
to arrive	to explain	to marry
to invite	to weigh	~~to rob~~

Match the verbs in the box to these nouns.

a o r r y b b e   = *robbery (to rob)*   **f** v r l a i r a   = ...
b o m r s c a o n p i = ...   **g** i t n i a v o n t i = ...
c a r m i a r e g   = ...   **h** g e w h i t   = ...
d u a e t r g m n   = ...   **i** p n e a l i o x a t n = ...
e o h e c c i   = ...

5 Complete each sentence by making changes to the word in **bold**.

a The designer had **invited** a large number of celebrities to his show.
The designer had sent .... a large number of celebrities for his show.

b There was great excitement when a famous footballer **arrived** wearing a skirt.
There was great excitement at .... a famous footballer wearing a skirt.

c The models had no **choice** about the clothes they wore at the show.
The models .... the clothes they wore at the show.

d Everyone in the audience heard the designer and one of his models **arguing**.
Everyone in the audience heard the .... the designer and one of his models.

e The designer gave an **explanation** for his use of only one colour for all his clothes.
The designer .... why he used only one colour for all his clothes.

Paris fashion show for men

→ See page 95 for Supplementary Activities.
More sentence transformation practice in Unit 3.

Writing

In the exam

In Part 1 of the Writing Test you will 'transform' five sentences by rewriting them with different words that give the same meaning. The beginning and end of each sentence is given. You must write no more than three words. This part tests your grammar.

In this unit

- Practice with key grammar
  – modal verbs
  – if and unless
- Spotting the mistakes
- Exam practice for Part 1

To start you thinking ... about school and college

1 Which subjects do you think will be most useful to study ten years from now and why? In pairs, you have two minutes to make a list of your Top Five (1 = most useful) from the subjects below, or you can choose some of your own subjects if you prefer.

engineering	cookery	computer sciences	art
English	health education	sport management	Chinese
law	yoga	history	the weather

Compare your list with others in the class. Are there any subjects that appeared on everybody's list?

Practice with key grammar

2 In this exercise you will practise rewriting sentences that include
- different modal verbs a–e
- *if* or *unless* f–g
(see Grammar File, page 110)

Here are some things that British schoolchildren said about their ideal school. Complete the second sentence so that it means the same as the first. All the words you need are in the box.

unless you	~~should~~	you don't
could choose	must have	ought to be
don't need/don't have		

In my ideal school ...

a It'd be a good idea to have laptops so we could work at home.
We __should__ have laptops so we could work at home.

b It's not necessary to do homework every night.
You .... to do homework every night.

c You wouldn't have to study subjects that you didn't like.
You .... the subjects you study.

d There would definitely be a swimming pool in my ideal school.
We .... a swimming pool.

e We should have a quiet room in the school for people who like silence.
There .... a quiet room in the school for people who like silence.

f You don't have to take an exam unless you want to.
If .... want to take an exam, you don't have to.

g In fact, you don't have to go to school at all, if you decide not to.
You don't have to go to school at all .... decide to.

Do you agree or disagree with these ideas? Is there one thing you would like in *your* ideal school or college?

40

Spotting the mistakes

3 Imagine a student has completed the sentences below, but (s)he has made a mistake every time. Correct the wrong part. Remember that the answers must have no more than three words.

a Everyone in my class is older than me.
I'm the ~~younger one~~ in my class. _youngest (one)_

b How long have you known your best friend?
When _have you met_ your best friend?

c I get on better with my Maths tutor than my science tutor.
I don't get on _well with_ my Science tutor as my Maths tutor.

d I don't think you should change courses in the middle of the term.
If I were you, _you shouldn't_ change courses in the middle of the term.

e I met my boyfriend at university.
My boyfriend and I _have met_ at university.

f The Music Department was given 10 million euros by a famous pop star.
A famous pop star _gives_ 10 million euros to the Music Department.

g People without university degrees don't usually have as many opportunities as graduates do.
Graduates usually have _many opportunities_ than people without university degrees.

h The interviewer asked me when I wanted to start work.
The interviewer asked: "When _you want_ to start work?"

i In most jobs, you can wear your own clothes to work.
In most jobs, you _don't must_ to wear a uniform.

j I haven't had a day off work for ages.
It's ages _that I haven't_ had a day off work.

k It's natural to work hard if you're the owner of a business.
It's natural to work hard if the business _belongs_ you.

l It's hard to explain his success in business.
It's hard to find _explaining_ his success in business.

m My boss lives quite near our house.
My boss doesn't _live a long way_ from us.

➜ **See page 95 for Supplementary Activities.**

Exam practice for Part 1

Exam tip

- Try and identify what is being tested – a tense, comparison, positive to negative, direct speech, etc.
- Remember you must only write one, two or three words.

Here are some sentences about work.
For each question, complete the second sentence so that it means the same as the first.
Use no more than three words.

Example:

0 I prefer studying in a library to studying at home.
I like studying in a library _more than_ studying at home.

1 What was Anne's reason for leaving her job?
Why .... her job?

2 David asked me if I liked my boss.
David asked, '............................ your boss?'

3 You can't compare my work with yours.
There is no .... my work and yours.

4 I don't think you should work at the weekends.
If I were you, I .... at the weekends

5 People work much harder than they need to.
People don't need to work .... they do.

Writing

UNIT 4 Short messages (1)

In the exam

In Part 2 of the Writing Test, you will write a short message of 35–45 words. The notes, cards, emails, etc. that you write test how well you can communicate three specific pieces of information.

In this unit

- How do you say it?
- What's missing?
- Adding more details

To start you thinking … about reasons for writing notes

1 Why do people write emails or letters? In pairs, you have two minutes to add five more reasons to the list.

to make an arrangement to meet, to invite someone to a party

How do you say it?

2 In the exam, you're given some information to include in your notes, cards or emails. For example, you may be told to *ask, invite, suggest* (see List A below).
List B gives some of the words you can write in your messages, in order to follow the instructions.
Match each instruction in A to a way of expressing it in B.

A	B
1 Invite someone	a Be careful!
2 Remind	b I'm sorry about …
3 Congratulate	c Why don't we …?
4 Say sorry	d Thanks a lot for … It was really …
5 Say 'no' to an invitation	e Great! I'd really like to …
6 Thank	f Don't forget …
7 Explain what happened	g Congratulations! You must be feeling …
8 Ask for information	h Would you like to come …?
9 Warn	i Hope you have / enjoy …
10 Make a suggestion	j I'd rather go / have …
11 Say what you prefer	k What happened was that …
12 Say 'yes' to an invitation	l I'm afraid I can't …
13 Wish someone good things	m What do you think I should …?
14 Ask for advice	n Can you tell me …?

What's missing?

3 Read the following notes, notices and cards. Write the missing line for each one.
For a–e use some of the phrases from column B in exercise 2.
For f–h use your own ideas.

42

a
Sorry!

I'm sorry about breaking your mirror. I'll buy you another one at the weekend.

b
Invitation

9.00 pm till late. Friends welcome!

c
Thanks

I had a really great time.

d
Good luck

I'm sure you'll do really well.

e
Remember

She'd be really angry if we forgot.

f
Lost

It's got my name on the front cover.

g
Phone message

He wants you to meet him outside the cinema at 8.

h
Great news

I'll tell you all about it next week.

Adding more details

4 In the exam, you're given the three points that you must include in your message. Look at this question and the example answer which follows it.

You went to a friend's house for dinner.
Write a card of 35–45 words to
- **thank him/her**
- **say what you enjoyed the most**
- **suggest another meeting**

Underline the words on the card that 'match' the three points you were asked to include.

Thanks
The cooking
Saturday, 28th?

Thanks a lot for a lovely evening on Sunday. I really enjoyed myself. Everything you made was great, particularly the soup. What about meeting again soon? Are you free on Saturday 28th? Give me a ring and let me know. (41 words)

Now read the following. Use the ideas that are given, and write between 35 and 45 words for each one.

a You want to invite a friend to stay with you for the weekend. **Write an email to**
- **invite him/her**
- **tell him/her what you can do together at the weekend**
- **remind him/her to bring the holiday photos**

Come for the weekend ....
Go to football match ....
Bring photos ....

b You spilt some coffee on your friend's book. **Write a note to**
- **apologise for the accident**
- **say how it happened**
- **say what you're going to do**

Sorry ....
Knocked it with elbow ....
Buy another ....

c A friend has offered to feed your goldfish while you're away. **Write a note for him/her to**
- **tell him/her when to feed the fish**
- **tell him/her where the fish food is**
- **tell him/her when you'll be home**

Once a day ....
Table in kitchen ....
Sunday, late ....

→ See page 95 for Supplementary Activities. More message writing practice in Unit 5.

Writing

In the exam

In Part 2 of the Writing Test, you will write a short message of 35–45 words. The notes, cards, emails, etc. that you write test how well you can communicate three specific pieces of information.

In this unit

- Keeping it short
- Including the right points
- Exchanging notes
- Exam practice for Part 2

To start you thinking … about messages

1 Txt talk (or text talk) is the quickest, cheapest and coolest way to send a message on your mobile. Are you a texpert? In pairs, see if you can work out these text messages.

  a TA4N   = <u>That's all for now.</u>   **d** CUL8r   = _____

  b CU   = _____   **e** WerRU? = _____

    (think of the pronunciation of each letter)   **f** Wan2Tlk? = _____

  c CU2nite = _____   **g** Thnx   = _____

Keeping it short

2 The messages you write in the exam must be between 35–45 words. Read this question.

> Your friend, Sarah, left a message for you. She wants to meet on Saturday, but Saturday is not possible for you.
> **Write an email to Sarah. In your email you should**
> - **say you aren't free on Saturday**
> - **tell her why**
> - **suggest another day to meet**
> Write 35–45 words for your email.

Look at this answer.

Hi, Sarah, thanks for your message. Sorry I wasn't in when you called – I was doing some shopping.
I'd love to see you, but I'm afraid Saturday's impossible.
It's ages since our last evening out together – we went to the theatre, do you remember?
Unfortunately, this weekend I've got to stay in and work. My exams are next week.
How about Saturday the 16th? I'll be able to relax then!
Ring me back over the weekend and tell me what you think. (82 words)

Which sentences can you cut to make it the right length (35–45 words)? Make sure you still include the three points above.

3 Read this question and the answer that follows it. Take out the extra sentences so that the email is the right length (35–45 words).

> Your friend works for a bank. It's possible that the bank is going to close the office where he works, and he may lose his job.
> **Send him an email of 35–45 words:**
> - **say you're sorry about his situation**
> - **suggest what he could do**
> - **ask him to tell you when he has more news**

Kenji
I haven't written earlier because I've been in Florence for a week on holiday. I'm really sorry to hear the news about your job. It'll be very sad if your office closes. But maybe they haven't made the final decision yet. Why don't you go and ask your boss what's happening, so at least you'll know? It's very difficult when people aren't really sure what's going on. Ring me as soon as you hear anything.
(76 words)

Including the right points

4 In the exam, it's important to include all three points in the question. You'll lose marks if you don't. Read this question and the answer that follows it.

> You've had to go out.
> **Write a note for your flatmate (in 35–45 words), telling her**
> • **where you've gone**
> • **how long you'll be out**
> • **what she should do before you return**

Natasha

Erika rang and asked me to go round to her house – she's got an exam tomorrow and needs my help. So I'm going to college first to pick up my notes. I'll cook supper, but could you start doing the vegetables while you're waiting?

Misha

a Which piece of information has been missed out? Write a sentence to include this.

b Which is the sentence that contains extra, unnecessary information? Cross it out.

Exchanging notes

5 In pairs, you're going to write notes to each other, and then reply to them.
Student A: Start with Situation 1.
Student B: Start with Situation 2.

Situation 1: You receive this note from your partner:

> .... and have you still got my Buffy video? I'd like it back please!

Student A

> Write a reply to your partner (in 35–45 words)
> • explain why you haven't returned the video
> • tell him/her if you liked it
> • offer to lend him/her one of yours

Student B

> Read the note you receive. Answer it (35–45 words).
> • say something about his/her explanation
> • reply to his/her offer of another video
> • give some news about a friend you both know

Situation 2: You're leaving school/college next term because your family are moving to another town.

Student B

> Write a note to your partner (35–45 words)
> • tell him/her about your move to another town
> • say how you feel about this
> • invite him/her to come and stay

Student A

> Read the note you receive. Answer it (35–45 words).
> • give your reaction to his/her news about moving
> • reply to his/her invitation
> • ask him/her to keep in touch

→ **See page 96 for Supplementary Activities.**

Exam Practice for Part 2

Exam tip

> • Make sure you include all three points that you're given. You'll lose marks if you don't include them all.

You receive a note from your friends, Sarah and David, inviting you to their engagement party on Saturday 23rd March.

Write a card to Sarah. In your card, you should
• **offer your congratulations**
• **say 'yes' to the invitation**
• **suggest meeting for lunch next week**
Write 35–45 words.

Writing

In the exam

In Part 3 of the Writing Test, you will write either an informal letter or a story in about 100 words.

In this unit

- Organisation of letters
- First and last lines
- The main message

To start you thinking … about feelings

1 **If you write a letter in the exam, you will often be asked to say how you feel about something – why you enjoy something, or which is your favourite, for example.**

Answer these questions:
- What's your favourite day of the week?
- What's your favourite time of year?
- What's your least favourite food?
- Who's your favourite sports person?
- What's your favourite item of clothing at the moment?
- What do you enjoy most/least about the weekends?
- Which CD or book would you really hate to lose?

2 **In pairs, compare with a partner. Do you have any answers which are the same? Find out the reasons for your partner's answers.**

e.g. *Why's spring your favourite time of year? Because it makes me feel happy.*

or *Why don't you like …?*

or *What's good/bad about …?*

Write some of the things you or your partner said.

a I really like .... because it makes me ....

b My favourite .... is/was .... because ....

c His/her least favourite .... is .... That's because ....

d The reason he/she enjoys .... is because ....

e The .... I like best/least is .... because ....

f I think .... is great because ....

g I don't really like .... because ....

h The thing I enjoy most about .... is ....

i .... doesn't interest me/her/him because ....

Organisation of letters

3

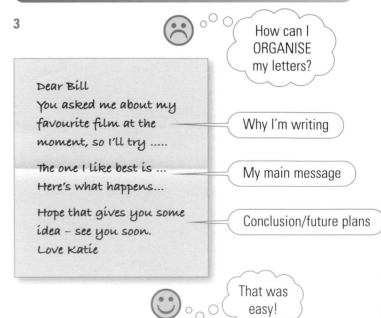

First lines …

4 The first line of your letter is very important because it tells the reader why you're writing.
Match the two halves of these sentences to make *first lines* of different letters.

Start …
1 The reason why I'm writing …
2 I'm really sorry …
3 Hi! Did you …
4 Thanks a lot …
5 I'm thinking of …
6 It's a long time since …
7 I really enjoyed …
8 It was great to …
9 You asked me …

… Continue
a … hear from you.
b … I last wrote to you.
c … to tell you about my last holiday.
d … hearing from you.
e … is to invite you to visit my town.
f … for your letter.
g … have a good holiday?
h … to hear about your accident.
i … coming to Japan soon.

… and last lines

5 A good last line will help the reader to feel positive about your letter.
Match the two halves of these sentences to make *last lines* of different letters.

1 I hope we'll be able to …
2 I'm looking forward to …
3 Hope to …
4 Give my …
5 Anyway, I must …
6 I'll speak …
7 Please write soon …
8 With …
9 Say …
10 That's all …

a … best wishes.
b … hello to Simon for me.
c … love to Chris.
d … and tell me what you think.
e … for now.
f … hearing from you soon.
g … stop now.
h … meet very soon.
i … hear from you soon.
j … to you before too long.

The main message

6 **You've looked at first and last lines. Now you need to think about the details that go in the middle paragraph(s) of letters.**
An English-speaking friend writes and says:

In your next letter, tell me all about the house or apartment you live in. Do you like it?

In pairs, ask and answer these questions to help you get ideas.

Where is your home? e.g. Is it in the middle of a city? Or in the suburbs?
What's it like? e.g. How big is it? Is it modern? Does it have a garden?
Who lives there? **How many** rooms has it got?
What about your room? Do you like it? **Why** (not)?
What's your favourite room? **Why**? **What**, if anything, would you like to change?

**Now complete this letter to your friend.
Look back to exercise 2 to help you describe your likes and dislikes. Write about 80 words.**

Dear Ed
You asked me to tell you about my home.
Well, ……………………………………………………
I hope one day you'll be able to come and visit me and then you can see everything for yourself!
Love Marina

→ See page 96 for Supplementary Activities.
More letter writing practice in Unit 7.

Writing

In the exam

In Part 3 of the Writing Test, you will write either an informal letter or a story in about 100 words.

In this unit

- Using the right verb tense
- Letter writing practice
- Further practice

To start you thinking … about comparing

1 🎧 When you write a letter, you may need to make a comparison between, for example, two films you've seen, or two people you know. First, listen to these nine different people. Who (a friend, a family member, etc.) or what (a sport, an activity, an event, etc.) do you think each speaker could be talking about? (There are no right answers!)

a ___swimming___   f _____
b _____   g _____
c _____   h _____
d _____   i _____
e _____

Listen again. Complete the gaps with the expressions of comparison the people use.

a I don't do it _____ I used to.
b People say _____ but I'm not so sure.
c It was _____ I thought.
d She seems _____ nowadays.
e It used to be _____ on a Saturday night.
f It's _____ the last one we had.
g It wasn't _____ people said.
h It's the _____ ever done.
i We've had _____ with it than we expected.

Use some of the different ways of comparing from sentences a–i above, and write sentences about yourself and your life.

your home town	the clothes you wear
your friends & family	using the Internet
your work or studies	spending money
your free time	your last holiday

e.g. I don't play volleyball as much as I used to.

48

Using the right verb tense

2 When you write a letter, it's important to use the right verb tense.

e.g. something that's finished – past tense
something now – present tense or present perfect
something in the future – *going to*, *will* or present continuous
(see Grammar File pages 104–107)

Read this letter from Jamie about his surfing holiday in Hawaii.
Fill in the gaps with the correct verb tense.
Use the verbs in brackets.

Dear Alicia

Well, here I (1) **am** (be), sitting in my father's flat in London and dreaming about Hawaii. I (2) _____ (get) back on Saturday but I (3) _____ (already plan) my next surfing holiday! The course I (4) _____ (do) in Hawaii (5) _____ (be) really fantastic and the instructors (6) _____ (help) us a lot with all the techniques for the big waves.

On the last night, we all (7) _____ (go) to a restaurant for our final meal together. It (8) _____ (be) quite sad to say goodbye. I really hope one day I (9) _____ (be) able to go back there.

Now I (10) _____ (stay) in London for a few days with Dad. We (11) _____ (just get) home after walking all over the city today and my feet hurt. Next week I (12) _____ (go) back to university – I'm looking forward to (13) _____ (see) all my friends again, but I wish I was back in Hawaii!

Take care.

Love Jamie

Letter writing practice

3 This exercise will give you the ideas that you're going to use in a letter.
Here is part of a letter Sabine received from Roger, an English-speaking friend.

> You said in your last letter that you wanted to do something different to get fitter. Sounds interesting! Have you started yet?

Now look at the pictures and talk together for a few minutes about what's happening in each one.

Think of two things *you* could start doing that would make you fitter.
Think of two things *you* could stop doing that would make you fitter.

In pairs, compare your ideas.

🎧 Listen to Sabine's reply to Roger. Number the pictures as you hear them being described.

Use the pictures in the correct order to help you write Sabine's letter. You don't need to write exactly what she said on the cassette.

> Dear Roger
> Well, I've started my new fitness programme. ....
> ....
> ....
> ....
>
> I hope you'll be able to see the difference when we next meet!
> Love Sabine

Further practice

4 Here is part of a letter you received from Gill, an English-speaking friend.

> I didn't feel very well at the weekend so I stayed at home and watched *Ice Storm* on DVD – much better than seeing it at the cinema, don't you think? Which do you prefer – watching films at home or going to the cinema?

Write your letter to Gill in about 100 words.

Before you begin, decide
- what you're going to say in the first sentence
- what your answer to her question is – which do you prefer? Why? Does it depend on the kind of film, or who you are watching it with, or when you want to watch it?
- what your last sentence will be

➡ See page 96 for Supplementary Activities.
More letter writing practice in Unit 8.

Writing

UNIT 8 Letters (3)

In the exam

In Part 3 of the Writing Test, you will write either an informal letter or a story in about 100 words.

In this unit

- Making a letter more interesting
- Spelling and punctuation
- What makes a good letter
- Exam practice for Part 3

To start you thinking … about plans

1 In a letter, you'll often need to write about your plans, or your feelings about something in the future. Write short answers to the following.

   a Name a city you'd like to visit before you're 30.

   b What are you going to do at the weekend?

   c What sort of job do you **not** want to do in the future?

   d Name one thing you're thinking of buying this week.

   e What (or who!) do you hope will disappear in the next five years?

   f Name one thing you're planning to do on your next holiday.

   g Do you think you'll get married in the next five years?

   In pairs, find out what your partner wrote by asking questions.

   e.g. Which city would you like to visit before you're 30?

2 What other plans have you got for the next five years? Write your ideas below.

   In the next five years …
   a I hope I'll
   b I'd like to
   c I don't want to
   d I don't think I'll
   e I'm planning to
   f I'm thinking of
   g I don't know if I'll

Making a letter more interesting

3 Read this letter from George to Charlotte about his holiday. It is correct, but it only gives some very basic information, so it's not very interesting. To make it a better letter, add some details. Use the notes and questions to help you.

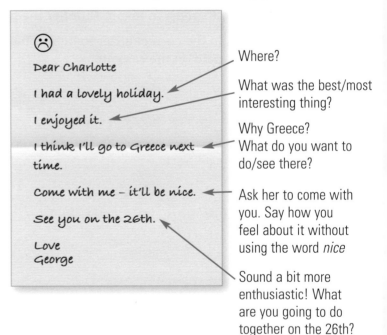

50

Spelling and punctuation

4 In the exam, a letter that doesn't have too many spelling or punctuation mistakes will make a good impression.

Read this letter from a student who lives in Scotland, to her penfriend. There are seven spelling mistakes in her letter and five mistakes in the punctuation. Make the corrections.

Dear Nathalie

You asked me how I usualy spend my summer holidays, and what I'm planing to do this year in july. I'm happy to tell you about this – it's something cheerful to think about now in febuary, when the wether is so cold and miserible. do you remember I told you about my grandmother, who lives in the country on an old farm. Every summer we go there and spend four wonderfull weeks riding horses, feeding the chickens and swiming in the lake. Its very cold water, but we still enjoy it! What are your plans for this summer? Looking forward to your next letter.
Love Fiona

This letter has no paragraphs, which makes it a bit difficult to read. Start a new paragraph when you want to introduce something new.

Divide Fiona's letter into three paragraphs.

What makes a good letter

5 Some students were asked to write a letter of about 100 words in reply to this:

... so that's what I'm planning to do. How about you? What are your ideas for the next five years of your life?

Read letters A and B.

A

Dear Clair
Hallo Clair! How are you?
I'm fine. How was your first trip to France? Did you enjoy in France? I wanted to hear the story of your trip to Paris.
Today I have finished my examination. And after the examination I talked with my friend about future dream. She had a lot of plan in the future. Her dream was to be a beautician. My dream is to be a doctor. Because I will help a lot of lives. Within five years I will be married and have two children. I'll live in the country with my hasband, my children and a cat. So that's what I'm planning to do. How about you? What are your ideas for the next five years of your life?
Yours Sumiko

B

Dear friend
I've received your letter just yesterday. I'm happy to know that you are optimist about your future.
I hope you can obtain the new job and realise your dream.
I'm in a particular moment this year. I decided to change office (how you know I don't like it). Then I'm trying to pass an exam – it's not easy to do so I must do my better. If I will pass the exam I will have more chance for my career. So I hope to stay in my city the next three years. Then it's possible to work abroad in an international office. I would like to go in some European country but I'm not deciding about it. How you can see my future is more unsure then your, but I'm happy to have a friend like you.

Yours sincerely
Masoud

In pairs, discuss what you think about these two letters and answer the questions below.

	Letter A	Letter B
1 Does it answer the question?		
2 Does it have a good beginning/ and a good end?		
3 Is it well organised?		
4 Does it use some different verb tenses?		
5 Is there any interesting vocabulary?		
6 Do the mistakes make it hard to understand the message?		

(see Appendix 1, marking criteria page 115.)

➜ See pages 96 and 97 for Supplementary Activities.

Exam practice for Part 3

Exam tip

- Use questions 1–6 above to remind you about what's important when you're writing a letter.

This is part of a letter you received from an English penfriend.

Do you use a mobile phone? What do you think about mobile phones in the future?

Now write a letter to this penfriend.
Write your letter in about 100 words.

Writing

UNIT 9 Story (1)

In the exam

In Part 3 of the Writing Test, you will write either an informal letter or a story in about 100 words.

In this unit

- Choosing the right past tense
- Getting started on the story
- What happened next – getting ideas

To start you thinking … about important moments

1 🎧 Listen to this woman telling her story about an important event in her life. Tick (✓) the picture which you think goes with her story.

2 Now think about something important that has happened in your life, or in the life of someone you know. Decide what you're going to say with the help of the questions below.

What was the big moment? ☐

How old were you at the time? ☐

Where did it take place? ☐

What happened? ☐

Why is/was it a big moment for you? ☐

Were you alone or with others? ☐

Was it a good thing that happened? ☐

Was it a surprise? ☐

How did you feel? ☐

Were there any problems? ☐

In pairs, tell each other your stories. As you listen to your partner, tick the questions (s)he chose to answer.

Choosing the right past tense

3 Look at these pictures which show what happened to a woman on a skiing holiday in Austria. The pictures are not in the right order for the story.

🎧 Listen to the woman, and as you listen, number the pictures in the order in which she talks about them. Listen a second time if necessary.

When you write a story, you'll need to use past tenses to describe what happened. (see Grammar File pages 104–106)

- Past simple   e.g. *At first I **thought** it was …*
- Past continuous e.g. *It **was raining** when I left …*
- Past perfect   e.g. *I'd never **seen** such a wonderful …*

Use the pictures to help you fill in the gaps in the woman's story.

The day I broke my leg

It **(1)** ..happened.... (happen) two years ago when I **(2)** .... (ski) in Austria. It was a horrible day because it **(3)** .... (snow) and I **(4)** .... (can't see) anything. I **(5)** .... (not/want) to ski but my friends said, "Come on. This is our last day. We must go." So I went. I **(6)** .... (not/ski) in conditions like that before so when my friends **(7)** .... (decide) to go right up to the top of the mountain, I **(8)** .... (not/join) them. After about half an hour by myself, I **(9)** .... (stop) because I was cold and wet. I **(10)** .... (get) into the cable car to go down to the village and my wonderful warm hotel when I **(11)** .... (slip) on some ice. I **(12)** .... (fall), and my skis **(13)** .... (fall) on top of me. I **(14)** .... (hear) a terrible noise and knew something bad **(15)** .... (happen). My leg was broken. What a way to end a holiday!

🎧 **Now listen again to check your answers.**

Getting started on the story

4 **When you write a story you want to make sure that the reader is interested from the start. Here are some 'beginnings' of different stories.**

In pairs, decide how you could continue the sentences. Use your own ideas but use the verb tense given.

a The house was quiet and I realised that __everyone had left.__ (past perfect)
b It was a hot sunny day and Martin .... (past continuous)
c Immediately I walked into the room I .... (past simple)
d I first met Marta when she .... (past continuous)
e When Anna heard Joe's voice on the phone, she knew .... (past perfect)
f Thomas was working at his desk .... (past simple)

5 **Below are some first sentences from different stories. Write the second line of each story. You can get ideas by thinking about answers to the questions in brackets.**

a David opened the letter nervously. (*Why?*) __He knew that his life might change because of it.__
b The woman stood outside the bank, looking at her watch. (*Why?*)
....
c I had a wonderful day last week. (*Who with? Which day?*)
....
d There was no moon that night so it was very dark. (*Where were you?*)
....
e It was a holiday that none of us will ever forget. (*What happened first? Was it good or bad?*)
....

What happened next – getting ideas

6 **In pairs, read the beginning and the ending of these stories. Together decide what happened in the middle. Then compare your stories with another pair.**

Story 1
Alex, Jon and Nick went to the beach for the day.   *What did they do there?*
   Why was money important?
....
Finally, they found a bank that was open.

Story 2
Two years ago, I decided to take karate lessons.   *Why?*
   What happened?
....
The woman told the police that I was a hero.   *Why?*

Now write one of the stories in about 100 words. Think about which verb tenses you can use.

➡ **See page 97 for Supplementary Activities. More story writing practice in Unit 10.**

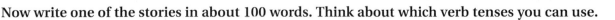

Writing

In the exam

In Part 3 of the Writing Test, you will write either an informal letter or a story in about 100 words.

In this unit

- Making longer sentences
- What happened next?
- Exam practice for Part 3

To start you thinking … about contrasts

1 In groups of three: tell each other the good and bad things that happened when Gino got lost in a foreign city. Use *Fortunately, …* and *Unfortunately, …* to continue the story:

Student A: Gino left his hotel to go for a walk. Unfortunately, he got lost.
Student B: Fortunately, he had a map with him.
Student C: Unfortunately, …

Continue as long as possible! Here's another story line for you to develop in the same way:

Carmen decided to go to the zoo. Unfortunately …

Making longer sentences

2 In the exam, you'll get better marks if you sometimes join two short sentences with a 'linker'.

Join each pair of sentences below with *although, because, but* and *so* (see Grammar File, page 108). Sometimes you'll have to change the order of the ideas.

a Marta got up early. She was tired.

Although Marta was tired, she got up early.

b It was warm. Adam decided to go for a walk.

It was warm so Adam decided to go for a walk.

3 You can also join ideas together by using different 'time' words like *when, as soon as, after,* etc. (see Grammar File page 108)

The story of Jack's visit to the dentist is in the wrong order. Read the first line (c) and then decide what the second line is and so on.
Each line (except the last one) ends with a 'linking' word, which will help you decide what comes next.

a	he heard it, he began to feel even worse. He tried to read something while
b	immediately felt sick because of the strange smell. The receptionist told him to wait until
c	**Jack slowly opened** the front door of the dentist's surgery and
d	we can see what the problem is this time." Jack's heart sank.
e	he was waiting but he couldn't concentrate on the boring magazines. After
f	Jack could hear a noise coming from the dentist's room. As soon as
g	sitting there for about ten minutes, he suddenly decided he wanted to go. But before
h	the dentist was ready for him. The waiting room was quiet and peaceful, but
i	he could escape, the dentist opened his door and said "Ah Jack, come in so

4 'Linkers' and verb tenses

You're going to complete the story of what happened to Felipe on Monday.
Join each pair of ideas with the word(s) given to make one sentence and put the
verbs into the right past tense form e.g *did, was doing, had done*.

On Monday I ...

a	can't find my trainers	– someone/steal them	(because)

... couldn't find my trainers because someone had stolen them.

b	burn the toast	– the smoke alarm/go off	(so)
c	have a row with my father	– he/come downstairs	(as soon as)
d	spill my coffee	– I/talk on the phone	(while)

In the evening I ...

e	can't watch TV	– I/break the remote control	(because)
f	play on the computer	– my brother/want to use it	(until)
g	have a row with my mother	– she/go to bed	(before)
h	It was a terrible day	– Tuesday/be even worse!	(although)

What happened next?

5 In pairs, look at the pictures and tell
the story.
The story begins:
*One cold winter evening, Andrea was
sitting at home ...*

Decide what happened in picture 6.
Tell your story to another pair.
How different are your stories?

Write your story (or someone else's)
in about 100 words.

➜ **See page 97 for Supplementary Activities.**

Exam practice for Part 3

Exam tip

- Look at the title or first line and ask yourself *who, what, where, when, why, how?* to help you think of some ideas.
- Leave yourself time to read your story after you've written it; imagine you're the examiner who is going to mark your writing. Check for: vocabulary; verb tenses; some longer sentences; paragraphs.

Your story has the title: "The best sports event I've been to".
Write your story in about 100 words.

Listening

UNIT 1 Multiple-choice pictures (1)

In the exam

In Part 1 of the Listening Test, you will listen to seven short recordings. After each one, you must answer a question by choosing the correct picture A, B or C.

In this unit

- Focus on numbers
- Practice with pictures

To start you thinking … about numbers

1 🎧 You'll hear some different numbers – times, dates, years, etc. Listen and write down exactly what you hear. You'll hear each one twice.

a	6 hours	g	
b		h	
c		i	
d		j	
e		k	
f			

2 In pairs, decide which numbers above answer the following questions. You may not agree with some of the answers!

a How many different languages are spoken in New York?

b How long does an average family spend on cleaning their home each week?

c How far does a person walk every year when making their bed?

d How much hair does a man grow on his face every day?

e What does a seven-year-old child in the UK get in pocket money each week?

f What per cent of Americans give their dogs birthday presents?

g How many calories a minute do you use up when kissing?

h How many babies are born every day?

i When were the plus (+) and minus (−) symbols first used?

j How long was the shortest war in history?

k What year did the Walt Disney Corporation allow its employees to have moustaches?

🎧 Find out if you've got the correct answers by listening to the recording.

Focus on numbers

3 🎧 In the exam, you'll need to be able to hear and understand numbers.

Listen to a woman giving some information about a school that teaches people to scuba dive. Write the answers to the following questions. They are all numbers, dates, times, etc.

a When did the school open?

b How many courses are there every year now?

c What's the maximum number of students in each class?

d When does the next course begin?

e When does the school day begin and end?

f How much is a one-week course?

g How much is the deposit?

Practice with pictures

4 🎧 **You will hear two people trying to arrange a date for a meeting. Listen and read.**

Man: We're trying to arrange a meeting to discuss our prices for next year. Is the 20th any good for you?

Woman: Sorry no. I can't do that or the following day so … what about the 22nd?

Man: It'll have to be, I guess. We need to announce the new prices before the 24th so we haven't got much choice.

Now answer the following.

	Yes	No
a Is the 20th OK for the man?	☐	☐
b Is the 20th OK for the woman?	☐	☐
c Can they meet on the 24th, or later?	☐	☐

so …

d What's the date for the meeting? Tick the correct answer.

20ᵗʰ ☐　　22ⁿᵈ ☐　　24ᵗʰ ☐

5 🎧 **Listen to a man talking about three different ways of travelling.**
The script is not written for you this time. Listen first, then answer the questions.

	Yes	No
a Does he have a car?	☐	☐
b Does he use it a lot?	☐	☐
c Is there any problem with the coach?	☐	☐

so …

d How does the man usually travel?

coach ☐　　car ☐　　train ☐

6 🎧 **Listen to a man and woman talking about sport and look at the pictures.**

A ☐　　**B** ☑　　**C** ☐

The correct answer is B. But the question is missing. Write the question that makes B the correct answer.

What .... ?

7 🎧 **For this recording, only two of the pictures are shown, and these two are the wrong answers. Draw the correct picture!**

Which toy is Chloe's favourite?

A ☐　　**B** ☐　　**C** ☐

8 🎧 **For numbers 8 and 9 there is no information given in the boxes.**
Listen to this man talking about his train journey. What time did he arrive?
Write the three times that you hear, and then tick the correct one.

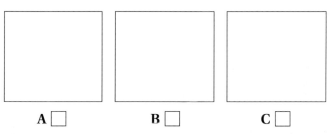

A ☐　　**B** ☐　　**C** ☐

9 🎧 **Listen to this conversation. Where are the man's keys? Write the three places that they talk about and tick the correct one.**

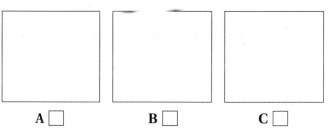

A ☐　　**B** ☐　　**C** ☐

➡ More listening practice with pictures in Unit 2.
See page 97 for Supplementary Activities.

Listening

In the exam

In Part 1 of the Listening Test, you will listen to seven short recordings. After each one, you must answer a question by choosing the correct picture A, B or C.

In this unit

- Listening for specific information
- Listening for general understanding
- What's right and what's wrong?
- Exam practice for Part 1

To start you thinking ... about the weather

1 **In pairs, complete the words to make the name of a strong wind.**

a You often hear it when you see lightning.   _ _ _ _ _ _

b You see a few of these high up in the blue sky.   _ _ _ _ _ _

c It's a gentle wind.   _ _ _ _ _ _

d The rain does this when it's coming down heavily.   _ _ _ _ _ _

e It's what the sun does.   _ _ _ _ _ _

f It describes frozen water.   _ _ _ _ _

g It's the opposite of cool.   _ _ _ _

h It was very ... and my hat blew off.   _ _ _ _ _

i It's the noun from 'hot'.   _ _ _ _

Listening for specific information

2 🎧 **In the exam, you'll need to listen for specific information. Here are three short recordings about different topics.**

a Listen to this conversation about the weather. Write down the four kinds of weather that the people talk about.

....

b Listen to this man talking about his family. Number these words in the order that he talks about them.

parents ....   cousins ....   mother ....   father ...1...

uncle ....   daughter ....   grandfather ....

c Listen to this woman talking about her dog. Circle the words in the box that you hear. Three of them are not mentioned.

tail	hair	legs	to feed	bark
(a walk)	bite	a bath	brushing	

Listening for general understanding

3 🎧 Listen in order to understand the general meaning of the whole recording – in other words, ask yourself 'What's it about?'

You'll hear three short recordings. For each one, decide what the people are talking about.

Tick (✓) the correct choice.

Recording 1

Are they talking about

going shopping ☐

or

cooking? ☐

Recording 2

Are they talking about

getting tickets for the cinema ☐

or

where to meet? ☐

Recording 3

Are they talking about

the best way to buy tickets for a concert ☐

or

finding out about a concert? ☐

Listen to recordings 4 and 5 twice. After the first listening, decide what the people are talking about. During the second listening, complete the missing information.

Recording 4

1st listening: What kind of accident did the woman have? ....

2nd listening: You knew the answer because of these words that the woman used:

'It just sort of .... hands.'

'The next thing I knew there were .... on ....'

Recording 5

1st listening: What's the woman talking about?

....

2nd listening: Which two words helped you decide?

the .... the ....

What's right and what's wrong?

4 🎧 In the exam, it's possible that two of the three pictures will show *some* correct information for the question, but only one picture will show *all* the correct things. Listen carefully.

Recording 6

You're going to listen to a man talking about two hotels.

Tick (✓) the information that's correct for **his** hotel.

main square	✓
modern	☐
balconies	☐
garden at back	☐
traditional	☐
by church	☐
view of mountains	☐

Recording 7

Now you're going to listen to a woman talking about her sister.

Tick (✓) the correct information about her sister.

wears jeans	☐
curly hair	☐
straight hair	☐
tall	☐
wears glasses	☐
wears skirts	☐

➡ **See page 97 for Supplementary Activities.**

Exam Practice for Part 1

Exam tip

- Look at the pictures very carefully. Remember, the person/people talking on the recording will probably mention all the different elements in the three pictures. But only one picture is 100% correct.

🎧 **You will hear the seven recordings in this unit again, but this time you're going to answer exam-style questions.**

There are seven questions in this part.

For each question there are three pictures and a short recording.

Choose the correct picture and put a tick (✓) in the box below it.

1 What is the man going to buy?

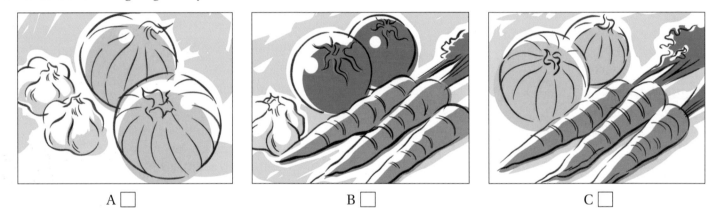

A ☐   B ☐   C ☐

2 Where are the two people going to meet?

A ☐   B ☐   C ☐

3 How did the woman find out about the concert?

A ☐   B ☐   C ☐

4 Which picture shows what happened?

A ☐   B ☐   C ☐

5 How did the film end?

A ☐   B ☐   C ☐

6 Which hotel did the man stay at?

A ☐   B ☐   C ☐

7 What does the woman's sister look like?

A ☐   B ☐   C ☐

Listening

In the exam

In Part 2 of the Listening Test, you will listen to one long recording and answer six multiple-choice questions.

In this unit

- Listening to the whole sentence
- Building up to multiple-choice

To start you thinking … about sounds

1 Look at these words.
   In pairs, take it in turns to say them.
   They should all sound different.

   hat ☐
   hut ☐
   hurt ☐
   heart ☐
   heat ☐ |
   hit ☐
   hot ☐
   height ☐

   a 🎧 Listen: you'll hear each word spoken twice, but not in the same order as above. Number the words as you hear them, 1–8.

   'Heat' is number 1.
   Individual words are difficult to understand sometimes, but when you hear the word in a sentence it usually becomes easier.

   b 🎧 Listen: you'll hear one of the above words in a sentence. Which word is it?

Listening to the whole sentence

2 🎧 **Listen: which of these two sentences do you think you hear?**

   a I've been working all morning.
   I've been walking all morning.

   It's difficult to be 100% sure because you don't know the situation, or context.

   Listen again. Now you'll hear some extra information which will help you choose the correct sentence.

   Now do the same with the following pairs of sentences. Tick (✓) which one you think you hear.

   b I'm going to live there …
   I'm going to leave there …

   c What was she doing …?
   What was he doing …?

   d We saw the men outside the station …
   We saw the man outside the station …

   e The championship medal was worn
   The championship medal was won

   f It's terrible that tigers are still shut …
   It's terrible that tigers are still shot …

   g It was a horrible test …
   It was a horrible taste …

   h Please eat the dessert …
   Please heat the dessert …

   i What made her think so fast? …
   What made her sink so fast? …

   j She likes peas …
   She likes peace …

k Is there a spare seat anywhere? …
Is there a spare sheet anywhere? …

l Could you wash the baby please? …
Could you watch the baby please? …

So, when you're listening to a recording, don't worry if you can't hear every word, the words around will help you understand the general meaning.

→ See page 98 for Supplementary Activities.

Building up to multiple-choice

3 🎧 You'll hear someone giving some information about a new leisure centre.
Look at these words in the box. Listen and circle the words that you hear.

exercise	facilities	get fit
member	swimming pools	café
fun	weekdays	tennis courts
courses	football	children

How many words have you not circled?

You're going to listen to the same recording again. First, look at these questions about the leisure centre.

a When did the leisure centre open?

b Do you have to be a member to use the centre?

c What does this centre have that other centres in the area don't have?

d When are the opening hours during the week?

e What other non-sports facilities are available?
a sauna, a steam-room, a .... , a .... , a place for kids to play and a ....

f What are the best ways to get there?

🎧 Now listen to the recording again and write a short answer for each question a–f.

4 Read these two-option multiple-choice questions; the questions are asked in the order that you hear the information on the recording, and they cover the same areas as a–f in exercise 3. You may want to hear the recording again. Circle the correct answer, A or B.

a People expected the Leisure Centre to open
  A last week.
  B eight months ago.

b The speaker particularly likes the fact that people
  A can pay for the swimming pools for a month.
  B don't need to pay a membership fee.

c The centre is very proud to have
  A six indoor tennis courts.
  B three swimming pools.

d On Saturdays, the Centre is open from
  A 7 am to 10.30 pm.
  B 6.30 am to 6 pm.

e On the ground floor you can
  A leave your children.
  B have a drink.

f What does the speaker complain about?
  A the car parking
  B the food

→ More multiple-choice practice in Unit 4.

Listening

In the exam	**In this unit**
In Part 2 of the Listening Test, you will listen to one long recording and answer six multiple-choice questions.	• Listening for specific information • Building up to multiple-choice

To start you thinking ... about detail

1 🎧 You will hear a man describing the scene outside a café. Read these six sentences. Listen and decide if each one is correct (✓) or incorrect (✗).

   a All the tables have flowers on them. ☐
   b Both the people are drinking. ☐
   c The woman isn't wearing a hat. ☐
   d The man's wearing jeans. ☐
   e There's a backpack on a chair. ☐
   f The waiter is carrying a tray. ☐

Listening for specific information

2 🎧 Some questions in the exam will test your understanding of detail or specific information.

   Look at the table below. You're going to hear a woman talking about five different cafés in the city of Oxford. As you listen, complete the information. Listen to the recording twice.

	Name	Where	Size	Food/drink	Who goes?	Anything special?
1	Queen's Lane Café	a	b	c ...., bacon, sausages & beans	d	Very busy
2	e	High Street	f	smoked salmon with champagne	g	h ....
3	Café Coco	15 minutes' walk from centre	i	Burgers, salads, traditional food	j	Read newspapers
4	Edgar's Café	k	Not given	l	people doing shopping	m ....
5	Freud's Café	Walton Street	n	Not given	o	It was a church and it has p ....

Building up to multiple-choice

3 🎧 You will hear part of the information about the cafés again.
First, in pairs, discuss what words could go in the gaps in sentences
a–e below. Then listen and complete the sentences with the exact words
used on the recording.

   a Queen's Lane Café is very popular with university students because they
   cook .... English-style .... there.

   b The Grand Café is quite a small place but it ....
   .... because the walls are covered in mirrors, which makes it
   really special. As you can probably guess, it's ....
   in the Grand Café.

   c It's really friendly in Café Coco. Nobody minds if you ....
   You can sit in comfortable chairs, read the newspapers, ... the world,
   and eat burgers or salads – or you could simply ....

   d Then there's Edgar's Café which is actually not particularly .... except it's right in the
   .... So you can imagine it's very .... with people doing their
   shopping – just to .... for a quick snack and a drink.

   e People walking past Freud's would never guess it was a café. It looks ....
   .... , which it was until about 20 years ago.
   What's interesting about this place is .... the food or drink,
   .... that they have live music there.

4 The information you wrote in exercise 3 above will help you to choose the correct answer,
   A, B or C, to these multiple-choice questions. Tick (✓) the correct answer. (If you have difficulty
   remembering, look back to exercise 3.)

   1 Students go to the Queen's Lane Café because   **A** ☐ it's small and friendly.
                                                          B ☐ they like the food.
                                                          C ☐ they can read there.

   2 The Grand Café is   **A** ☐ bigger than it looks
                               B ☐ smaller than it appears.
                               C ☐ more expensive than you think.

   3 In Café Coco you   **A** ☐ can sit there for a long time.
                              B ☐ have to eat something.
                              C ☐ shouldn't talk too much.

   4 The best thing about Edgar's Café is   **A** ☐ the food it serves.
                                                  B ☐ where it is situated.
                                                  C ☐ the fact that you sit outside.

   5 The surprising thing about Freud's Café is   **A** ☐ the music that is played there.
                                                        B ☐ the number of people who go there.
                                                        C ☐ the style of the building.

➜ See page 98 for Supplementary Activities.
More multiple-choice practice in Unit 5.

Listening

UNIT 5 Multiple-choice questions (3)

In the exam

In Part 2 of the Listening Test, you will listen to one long recording and answer six multiple-choice questions.

In this unit

- Listening to longer texts
- Dealing with multiple-choice questions
- Exam practice for Part 2

To start you thinking … about China

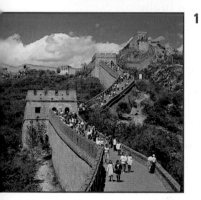

1 In pairs, how much do you know about China? Choose the correct answer.

a On average, how many people are born in China each year? **A** 12.79m **B** 5.62m **C** 14.34m

b What's the largest city? **A** Beijing **B** Hong Kong **C** Shanghai

c Which has the biggest land area? **A** Canada **B** Russia **C** China

d Which is the flag of China? **A** [flag] **B** [flag] **C** [flag]

e What did the Chinese not invent? **A** CD ROM **B** toothbrush **C** compass

f Which is the third longest river? **A** Amazon **B** Nile **C** Yangtze

g Which animal doesn't live there? **A** elephant **B** tiger **C** giant panda

Listening to longer texts

2 🎧 **You will hear Simon talking about his holiday in China. Look at the following multiple-choice questions. After each one there are two choices given and they are both *wrong*. Write the correct choice. The recording will be stopped to give you time.**

a On the first night in Beijing, Simon **A** had a party.
   B went to some temples.
   C watched some fireworks.

b At the Great Wall, Simon was unhappy about **A** the size.
   B ....
   C the colours.

c The Terracotta Warriors are amazing because **A** they were made for an Emperor.
   B there are so many of them.
   C ....

d What particularly interested Simon in Shanghai? **A** ....
   B the number of shoppers
   C the western-style buildings

e The weather in Guilin was **A** hot.
   B sunny.
   C ....

f In Hong Kong, Simon took the opportunity to **A** go for a boat trip.
   B do some shopping.
   C ....

Dealing with multiple-choice questions

3 🎧 **You will hear a woman talking about five different films. Listen to what she says about each film and then answer a question.**

a *The Wizard of Oz*
What does the woman like best?

b *The Lord of the Rings*
What negative point does the woman mention?

c *Monsoon Wedding*
How does the film make her feel?

d *The Others*
How does this film compare with other horror movies?

e *Phantom of the Rue Morgue*
How does the film compare with the book?

🎧 **Now for each question f–j, put a tick (✓) in the correct box. Your answers to the questions above should help you. Listen to the recording again if you need to.**

f In *The Wizard of Oz*, what did the woman particularly enjoy?
   A the scenery ☐
   B the music ☐
   C the main actress ☐

g The only problem with *The Lord of the Rings* is
   A the length ☐
   B the story ☐
   C the special effects ☐

h What does the reviewer say about *Monsoon Wedding*?
   A It made her laugh. ☐
   B It told a true story. ☐
   C It put her in a good mood. ☐

i What is different about *The Others*?
   A the servants are never seen ☐
   B the speed of the action ☐
   C the ending is very frightening ☐

j According to the reviewer of *Phantom of the Rue Morgue*
   A The film is better than the book. ☐
   B The film and the book are equally good. ☐
   C The book is better than the film. ☐

➡ **See page 98 for Supplementary Activities.**

Exam practice for Part 2

Exam tip

If you find the A, B, C multiple-choices more confusing than helpful, think about how you would answer in your own words – then look again at the A, B, C choices and find the one that matches your idea most closely.

🎧 **You will hear someone talking about dance marathon competitions.**
For each question, put a tick (✓) in the correct box.

1 The main reason why people entered dance marathons was
   A to get a job. ☐
   B to win some money. ☐
   C to have free meals. ☐

2 At all dance marathons, the dancers had to
   A stay awake. ☐
   B rest for 15 minutes. ☐
   C keep moving. ☐

3 The most successful dancers were
   A those with the best style. ☐
   B those who danced the longest. ☐
   C those the audience liked best. ☐

4 The audience gave the dancers
   A presents. ☐
   B money. ☐
   C drinks. ☐

5 The New York dance marathon in 1940 finished when
   A the police arrived. ☐
   B the dancers became ill. ☐
   C the organisers moved the dancers. ☐

6 The speaker thinks the film *They Shoot Horses, Don't They?* is
   A too long. ☐
   B quite cheerful. ☐
   C very good. ☐

Listening

In the exam

In Part 3 of the Listening Test, you will listen to one long recording and fill in six gaps in a text. You need to write one or more words in each space. Spelling should be recognisable, but if a word is dictated, the spelling must be correct.

In this unit

- Writing down messages
- Spotting the mistakes

To start you thinking ... about spelling

1 🎧 In this part of the Listening Test, it's possible that you'll hear the spelling of a name or an address. You have to write it down correctly.
Listen to these people spelling. Write down what they say.

a ....   **b** 59 .... Avenue

c ....   **d** ....

In pairs, take it in turns to spell and write down:

your full name
the first name of your mother or father
the address of your school/college
the name of a singer/actor/writer/sports person you like

You will also be asked to spell a name in the Speaking Test.

➜ **See page 98 for Supplementary Activities.**

Writing down messages

2 🎧 First listening: general understanding
Carole has just checked her voicemail. She has five messages.
Read the questions, then listen to her messages. There will be a pause between each message for you to answer the questions. Circle the message number. Sometimes there is more than one answer.

Which caller

apologises for a mistake?	1	2	3	4	5
asks Carole to ring back?	1	2	3	4	5
is a family member?	1	2	3	4	5
invites Carole to something?	1	2	3	4	5
talks about holiday plans?	1	2	3	4	5

🎧 **Second listening: complete the missing information.**

Message 1

From: Josie
About: TV programme
Name: ....
When: .... tonight
Channel: ....

Message 2

From: ....
About: dinner
New day: ....
Action: ....

Message 3

From: Elena
About: ....
When: ....
Where: ....

Message 4

From: Margrit
When: .... at ....
About: ....
Prices: ....
Action: .... on ....

Message 5

From: ....
About: ....
Action: ....

3 In pairs, you're going to leave and receive voicemail messages. Sit back to back with a partner. Take it in turns to ring each other.

Student B: Go to page 103.

Student A: Ring your partner's voicemail and leave a message. Your partner will write it down.

- give your name
- ask her/him to come to the cinema on Saturday
- tell her/him where to meet you

Now it's your turn to receive a message. Write it down.

Spotting the mistakes

4 🎧 Somebody at Dawson Holidays is listening to the answerphone after the weekend. Listen to this message and look at the form below. The missing information has already been filled in, but six of the nine points are wrong. Correct the wrong information.

Ꭰawson Holidays

Message for: **(1)** *Customer Complaints Manager*
From: **(2)** *Jason Thatchar*
 201 Barnsley Drive, Cambridge
Holiday ref: **(3)** *RW/37590*
Holiday destination: *Bahamas*
Where they stayed: **(4)** *Hotel Tropicana*
Complaint: *We changed their hotel two days before departure.*
 Problems with new hotel:
 (5) *not near* *beach and too far from capital city.*
Complaint: *Thinks we should give more information to customers.*
 His holiday was in **(6)** *June during the* **(7)** *hurricane season.*
 Rained for **(8)** *14 days* *.*
Action: *Wants us to* **(9)** *call as soon as possible.*

➔ **More gap-filling practice in Unit 7.**

Listening

In the exam

In Part 3 of the Listening Test, you will listen to one long recording and fill in six gaps in a text. You need to write one or more words in each space. Spelling should be recognisable, but if a word is dictated, the spelling must be correct.

In this unit

- Completing a form
- Completing notes
- Exam practice for Part 3

To start you thinking … about appearing on TV

1 Read this advertisement.

Want a challenge? Win 1m euros

Granta TV is looking for 12 people to spend three months together on a small, deserted island in the Pacific Ocean. The whole experience will be made into a TV programme. During your time on the island, you will take part in competitions and challenges and the final winner will get 1m euros.
Interested? Fill in an application form and send it to Granta TV.

In pairs, discuss the following questions.

a Would you like to do it? Why/ Why not?

b How would you feel about being filmed for three months?

c What would worry you the most about the experience?

d Have you ever seen any programmes like this on TV?

e Does the best person usually win in these situations?

Completing a form

2 In the Listening Test you may have to fill in a form.
Imagine you've decided to apply to Granta TV to join the group. What would you say about yourself? Fill in the application form below.

> **Granta TV Survival Challenge**
> **Application Form**
> Name ....
> Age ....
> Marital status ....
> Present job ....
> Sports you do ....
> Useful interests ....
> Any fears ....
> How would you rate your fitness?
> 1 – average; 3 – good; 5 – Olympic standard
> 1   2   3   4   5

3 🎧 Now listen to Clare from Granta TV leaving a voicemail message for a colleague about another application form she's received.
Fill in the missing information in the numbered spaces. You may need to hear the message twice.

> **Granta TV Survival Challenge**
> **Application Form**
> Name   Darius Gallagher
> Age   **(1)** ....
> Marital status   **(2)** ....
> Present job   **(3)** ....
> Sports you do   **(4)** ......, wind-surfing,   &
> Useful interests **(5)** cooking, boat-building &
> Any fears   **(6)** ....
> How would you rate your fitness?
> 1 – average; 3 – good; 5 – Olympic standard
> 1   2   3   4   5

70

Completing notes

4 Look at these pictures of theme park rides. What do you feel about them? Have you ever been on one? Would you do it again?

🎧 You will hear a woman giving some information about two exciting new rides at Britain's theme parks.
Fill in the missing information in the numbered spaces.

NAME OF RIDE:	Air
NAME OF THEME PARK:	Alton Towers
COST TO BUILD:	(1) ....
SPEED OF RIDE:	(2) .... kph
OPENING TIMES:	9.30 am to 7.00 pm
DATE PARK CLOSES:	(3) ....
COST OF TICKET:	£20 for children
	£25 for adults
	Everything includod cxcept
	(4) ....
	For hotel information ring
	(5) ....

NAME OF RIDE:	Colossus
NAME OF THEME PARK:	Thorpe Park
COST TO BUILD:	£10m, that is (6) ....
	for each loop
SPEED OF RIDE:	112kph
HOW LONG IT LASTS:	(7) ....
COST OF TICKET:	(8) .... for children
	£23 for adults; if you book
	in (9) .... it's cheaper
SEND COMMENTS TO:	John (10) ....

Which ride do you think sounds the best? Take a vote in your class.

→ See page 99 for Supplementary Activities.

Exam practice for Part 3

Exam tip

- The questions are in the same order as the information on the recording
- If you miss something the first time, remember you'll hear the recording again
- Usually you don't have to write more than one word in each gap

🎧 You will hear part of a radio programme about Mark Foster, a champion swimmer.
For each question, fill in the missing information in the numbered space.

Mark Foster: record-breaking swimmer

Facts

Has won a total of 31 medals including (1) ....
gold medals.

His swimming distance is (2) .... for freestyle and butterfly.

Background

It was his (3) .... who made him learn to swim.

Thinks of swimming as his (4) ....

Training

Trains every day except (5) ....

Before a competition, changes what he eats.

Diet includes a lot of (6) .... as well as fresh fruit & vegetables.

For competition

Needs power over short distances.

Races only take between (7) .... and 23 seconds.

Listening

In the exam

In Part 4 of the Listening Test, you will listen to a long dialogue and decide whether six statements about the dialogue are correct or incorrect. Some of the statements will be about the opinions and attitudes of the speakers.

In this unit

- Listening for key words
- Writing the statements

To start you thinking … about friends

1 What makes a good friend? In pairs, decide the importance of the following qualities and number them from 1 to 6 (1 = the most important).

A good friend is someone who …

	Importance 1–6	Who says it? (exercise 2)
a likes doing the same things as you.	....	....
b you can talk to about anything.	....	....
c understands you very well.	....	....
d you can have a good laugh with.	....	....
e you can depend on.	....	....
f is always happy to see you.	....	....

➡ **See page 99 for Supplementary Activities.**

2 🎧 Now listen to six people talking about their good friends. Each person refers to one of the points above, but they use different words to say it. Write the name of the speaker in the column 'Who says it?'

1 Jenny   2 Rob   3 Renate   4 Marcus   5 Zoe   6 Jack

Listening for key words

3 🎧 In this part of the exam, you need to be able to identify the important words and phrases that tell you whether a statement is correct or incorrect. Listen to the same six people talking about something important in their lives.

First listening: Who or what are they talking about?
Second listening: Write two or three key words which help you to find out what they are talking about.

	Who / What are they talking about?	Key words
Jenny	her bed	little table next to me; duvet
Rob		
Renate		
Marcus		
Zoe		
Jack		

4 Look at the sentences below about the same speakers. For each speaker, decide which sentence is right and which is wrong. You may need to listen to the recording again.

Speaker 1 – Jenny

a Jenny uses this place to escape to.   Yes/No

b Nobody knows about Jenny's special place.   Yes/No

Speaker 2 – Rob

c Rob thought that people would be surprised by his hobby.   Yes/No

d Rob's friends thought his hobby was rather strange.   Yes/No

Speaker 3 – Renate

e Darren stole some of her important files.   Yes/No

f Renate thought the situation would improve when Darren left. Yes/No

Speaker 4 – Marcus

g He liked it immediately he got it.   Yes/No

h Marcus feels it brings him luck.   Yes/No

Speaker 5 – Zoe

i Zoe would like to see more of these people.   Yes/No

j They help each other.   Yes/No

Speaker 6 – Jack

k Jack was unhappy about lending it to Maria.   Yes/No

l This event hasn't changed Jack in any way.   Yes/No

Writing the statements

5 🎧 This exercise will help you to understand the connection between what you hear and the statements you read. You will hear four short conversations. You can also read what is said. Listen to the first conversation. The sentences below it are true/false statements about the conversation.

In pairs, listen and write either a true or false statement for conversations 2–4.

Conversation 1

> Man: You're looking very well! Been away?
> Woman: Yes – but on business. I really enjoy these trips – I just love hearing different languages around me, and all the colours, and smells, and the food …
> Man: But you still had to work, didn't you?
> Woman: Of course, but I don't mind that.

Your sentence: The woman likes going on business trips.   (Yes)

OR   The woman doesn't like working on business trips.   (No)

Conversation 2

> Woman: Did you enjoy the film?
> Man: No, not really. I thought it was too long, not very funny and the acting was just bad. It looked good though, particularly the scenes under water.

Your sentence: The man _____ Yes/No

Conversation 3

> Young boy: What's that music, grandma?
> Grandmother: Beethoven's 5th symphony.
> Boy: Do you like it?
> Grandmother: Well, I wouldn't play it if I didn't like it, would I? I know you think I'm boring when it comes to music but I know what I like, and I like lots of different music from Beethoven to the Beatles.
> Boy: Who are the Beatles?

Your sentence: The boy's grandma _____
_____ Yes/No

Conversation 4

> Man: I really can't see why people spend so much just to get a designer name on their jeans – unless of course they're better made, or better quality material. And anyway, everybody knows half of them are cheap copies, not the real thing at all. I prefer to spend my money on other things.

Your sentence: The man _____ Yes/No

Write your sentences on a piece of paper and give them to another pair of students in your class. Decide if the answer for the sentences you receive is Yes or No.

→ More True/false practice in Unit 9.

73

Listening

In the exam

In Part 4 of the Listening Test, you will listen to a long dialogue and decide whether six statements about the dialogue are correct or incorrect. Some of the statements will be about the opinions and attitudes of the speakers.

In this unit

- Matching statements to what you hear
- Getting the right answer
- Exam practice for Part 4

To start you thinking … about taking time off

1 **Imagine you've finished all your exams and you have six months free. What will you do?**

   a go backpacking in Thailand?

   b work, for no pay, helping an animal organisation in Kenya

   c go sailing around the world in a traditional sailing ship

   d live in a foreign country in order to learn another language

   e find a job in your home town in order to earn as much money as possible

   f walk from the top to the bottom of South America

   g learn a useful skill, e.g. website design, how to play the guitar, etc.

   h borrow some money and start your own business.

   Put these in order from 1–8 (1 = would really like to; 8 = no thanks).

   In pairs, tell each other your order, and give your reasons.

Matching statements to what you hear

2 **In the exam, you need to decide whether the written statements are a correct summary of what you've heard.**

   🎧 **You will hear a conversation between two friends, Joe and Peter. Listen and write down the exact words you hear to complete these sentences. The recording will be stopped to let you do this.**

   a Peter: We'll see. I _____ _____ _____ get the mark I need for college.

   b Peter: In ten days. I _____ to get there.

   c Joe: I think _____ _____ _____ as long as possible.

   d Peter: I'd hoped you'd be able to but I know you _____ _____ _____ and …

   e Joe: I'm only joking. _____ _____ _____ have a drink.

   Now read the statements below. They describe some of the things Joe and Peter talked about but they're not in the same order as on the recording.

   Match these statements to the sentences a–e.

   1 Peter *understands* why Joe can't come with him.

   2 Joe *suggests* going for a drink.

   3 Peter is *unsure* about his exam results.

   4 Joe *encourages* Peter to stay in India.

   5 Peter is *looking forward* to going to India.

3 🎧 **You will hear three short conversations. They give you more practice in matching written statements to what you hear.**

   As you listen, fill in the missing words. The recording will be stopped to let you do this. Then decide which statement is right and which is wrong.

74

Conversation a: Nick and Andrea

'… why I needed it and she'd _____ _____ it.'

Carolyn promised to lend Andrea
some money.   **Yes/No**

Carolyn agreed to consider lending
Andrea some money.   **Yes/No**

Conversation b: Jamie and Ivana

'I wish I _____ _____ _____ tell her.'

Jamie doesn't want to tell Ivana
the news.   **Yes/No**

Jamie refuses to tell Ivana the news.   **Yes/No**

Conversation c: Marta and Sam

'Oh _____ _____ Sam, that'd be really kind.'

Marta asks Sam to post the letter
for her.   **Yes/No**

Marta accepts his offer to post
the letter.   **Yes/No**

Getting the right answer

4 In the exam, if you're not sure whether a
   statement is correct or incorrect, try changing
   the statement into a question – it may help.
   First, read the two statements below. Then
   change them into question forms.

   a Martina is interested in the sports programme
         on TV.
         Is Martina _____? **Yes/No**

b Martina feels unhappy about some animals
      living in cages.
      Does Martina _____? **Yes/No**

🎧 Now listen to Alex and Martina talking about
zoos and safari parks and answer questions *a*
and *b*. Stop the recording at the tone.

Change the sentences below into questions. Then
listen to the rest of the conversation and answer
your questions Yes or No.

c In Alex's opinion, it's necessary to keep animals
      in cages.
      Does Alex _____? **Yes/No**

d Martina already knows something about
      Woburn.
      Does Martina _____? **Yes/No**

e Martina thinks that your car can be damaged if
      you visit Woburn.
      Does Martina _____? **Yes/No**

f Alex agrees with Martina that some things
      about the park are quite funny.
      Does Alex _____? **Yes/No**

g In Martina's opinion, the weather is right for
      this kind of trip.
      Does Martina think _____? **Yes/No**

h The final decision is OK for both speakers.
      Is the _____? **Yes/No**

➡ **See page 99 for Supplementary Activities.**

Exam practice for Part 4

Exam tip

- Before the first listening, underline the key words in the statements e.g. time
  expressions like *at first*, *next year* or opinions like *Alex agrees that* … etc.
- The statements are in the same order as the information on the recording
- If you have difficulty deciding whether a statement is true or false, change it
  into a question – it sometimes helps you to understand things better

🎧 **Look at the six sentences for this part.**
You will hear a conversation between two college students, Mary and Jack, about a mobile phone.
Decide if each sentence is correct or incorrect.
If it is correct, put a tick (✓) in the box under A for YES. If it is not correct, put a tick (✓) in the box under B for NO.

		A YES	B NO
1	Mary's friends have had similar problems to Jack's.	☐	☐
2	Jack thinks it was someone else's fault.	☐	☐
3	Jack knows the thief's name.	☐	☐
4	Mary encourages Jack to report the crime.	☐	☐
5	Jack is unhappy about security at college.	☐	☐
6	Mary makes a suggestion that might help catch the thief.	☐	☐

Speaking

In the exam

In Part 1 of the Speaking Test, you must answer questions about yourself. This part lasts about two to three minutes.

In this unit

- Spelling
- Getting and giving personal information
- Exam practice for Part 1

To start you thinking … about the pronunciation of letters

1 **Say these letters aloud.**

a	as in	M**ay**		r	pronounced	'**are**'
e	as in	**e**ven		u	pronounced	'**you**'
g	as in	**jea**ns		v	as in	'**ve**al'
i	as in	**i**ce		w	pronounced	'**double you**'
j	as in	**ja**il		x	as in	'**ex**ercise'
k	as in	**Ka**te		y	pronounced	'**why**?'
q	pronounced	'**queue**'		z	to rhyme with	'**bed**'

🎧 **Listen and repeat.**

Spelling

2 **During the first part of the Speaking Test you will be asked to spell a word.**
Student A: Complete the sentences in Set 1 and Set 2 with *one* word.
Student B: Look at page 103 and do the same.

Student A: Set 1

a Have you had your _ _ _ _ cut? It looks different.
b Can I make an _ _ _ _ _ _ _ _ _ _ _ to see the doctor, please?
c You can breathe through your mouth or your _ _ _ _ .
d The opposite of 'boring' is _ _ _ _ _ _ _ _ _ _ _ .
e The biggest _ _ _ _ _ _ _ in the world in land area is Russia.

Student A: Set 2

a A large, grey animal with a trunk for a nose is an _ _ _ _ _ _ _ _ .
b There are 365 days in a _ _ _ _ .
c The opposite of 'innocent' is _ _ _ _ _ _ .

d Do you _ _ _ _ if I ask you a question?
e The sister of your mother is your _ _ _ _ .
f When you get married you usually wear a _ _ _ _ on your finger.
g The 11th month in the calendar is _ _ _ _ _ _ _ _ .

In pairs, when you're both ready, dictate the first letter of the words you wrote to your partner who will write the letters down.
Together re-arrange the letters in each set to make the names of two countries.

You and your partner now have the name of four countries. These countries are the places where:

- football was first played in 200BC
- a kind of basketball was common in the 10th century BC
- bowling (but only with nine pins) was played in the 17th century
- baseball was first written about in 1700

Match the country to the sport.

3 In pairs, take it in turns to spell these names and places aloud.

F-a-b-r-i-c-e   J-a-v-i-tt-e

S-a-s-k-a-t-oo-n   Q-u-e-b-e-c

🎧 Listen, and check your pronunciation.

Now tell your partner how to spell:
- your surname
- the place where you were born or live now
- the first name of someone else in the room

Getting and giving personal information

4 The examiner wants to know some information about you (now, in the past and in the future). He/she will use direct questions, e.g.

Can you/Did you … or What do/When are ….

Or more indirect ways, e.g.

– Tell me something about … or We'd like to know something about…

Tick (✓) if you can answer 'yes' to any of these questions:

Do you have an older brother? ☐

Do you usually walk to college or to work? ☐

Have you moved house or apartment recently? ☐

Did you go abroad for your last holiday? ☐

Can you play a musical instrument? ☐

Do you ever read in bed? ☐

Are you going to do any sport this week? ☐

Do you drink tea for breakfast? ☐

Are you learning to drive at the moment? ☐

Would you like to live in another country? ☐

Do you like chocolate ice cream? ☐

In pairs, use the ideas above to tell your partner about yourself. Be ready to say more than just one sentence.

e.g. I've got an older brother. (Is there anything more you can say about him?) He's 23 and his name's Sven.

5 🎧 Listen to this conversation between an examiner and one student, Bianca.

These are the ways the examiner asks for information. Number them in the order you hear them:

Where are you … ? ☐	Have you … ?	☐
Tell me something …☐	Could you … ?	☐ 1
What do you … ? ☐	Where would you … ? ☐	

Circle the topics that Bianca talked about.

free time   **SPORT**   *travel*

family   *her future*   music

reading   **FILMS**   her friends

job/studies   TV   English

Choose three of the other topics and write a question for each one, e.g. What sport do you do? In pairs, ask and answer each other's questions.

6 Below is a summary of the kind of language you'll use in this part of the Speaking Test. Complete these sentences with information about yourself.

> I'm …
> I come from …
> I was born in …
> At the moment I'm working/studying …
> I live …
> My family …
> In my free time, I enjoy …
> One day I'd like to …
> In the future I'd like to …/ I'm thinking of …/ I'm going to …

➡ **See page 99 for Supplementary Activities.**

Exam practice for Part 1

Exam tip

- Say a bit more than 'yes' or 'no' to questions like *Do you …? Are you…?*
- Be ready for questions about your 'present', 'past' and 'future'

🎧 Now it's your turn to take part in a Speaking Test. Listen: you will hear an examiner asking questions to two students (you and your partner).

In pairs, one of you is Student A and the other is Student B. Listen and speak your answers to the examiner's questions. Pause the recording after each question to give you time to answer.

If you want to practise this again without the tape, use the tapescript on page 141, and say your answers again.

Speaking

In the exam

In Part 2 of the Speaking Test, the examiner gives you a visual to look at and describes a situation. You discuss it with your partner and decide what to do. You have two or three minutes.

In this unit

- Yes, but …
- Matching people and things
- Talking about 'needs'

To start you thinking … about what some people might do

1 Write down the names of five or six people who are important in your life.
Now read these different things that people do:

- complain in a restaurant
- travel on a bus without paying
- tell someone's secret
- not wait in a queue for the cinema
- drop litter in the street
- say it was them who broke a glass

- take souvenirs from a hotel
- lie about their age
- eat raw fish
- organise a 'surprise' party for someone
- read someone else's diary or letters
- not tell a friend that their new sweater looks terrible

In pairs, tell each other if you think any of your five or six people would or wouldn't do these things and explain why.

e.g.

> I think/don't think my sister would lie about her age because …

> I'm sure my friend Marco would (never) … because

Yes, but …

2 In this part of the Speaking Test, it's important for you *both* to give your ideas and opinions about things.
In this exercise you can practise saying what you think, and also giving a different opinion.
In pairs, look at these pictures of different methods of transport.

Student A: Say something that you think is good or bad about one of these methods of transport.
Student B: Continue the conversation with 'Yes, but …' and then something different from A.

> comfortable expensive convenient
> in bad weather crowded relax
> take you door-to-door good exercise quick

e.g. A: (good point) I like trains because you can relax on them.
 B: (bad point) Yes, but sometimes the station is a long way from your home.
Or A: (bad point) I don't think trains are very good because they're expensive.
 B: (good point) Yes, but usually they're very quick.

Matching people and things

3 What makes a good holiday? Put the following points in order of importance for you. Number them from 1–10 (1 = most important).

good weather	sightseeing
people	sports activities
culture	peace and quiet
nightlife	food
adventure	scenery

In pairs, compare your ideas. Be ready to say *why* something is important or not important for you.

e.g. Sports activities are the most important for me because I like being active and doing things.

Look at the points again. Do you think the order of importance would be different for your parents? Use the language in the box to help you talk about this.

> Useful language: What would your parents like?
> 1 They might choose … (because) …
> 2 I think … is important/good/right (for them) (because) …
> 3 I don't think … is a good idea (because) …
> 4 They'd probably like / enjoy … (because) …
> 5 … would be good/better/best for them (because) …

4 In this part of the exam, you and your partner are given a picture sheet. You have to discuss the points for and the points against the various ideas/objects/activities shown and decide which is the best one for the situation.

A travel magazine has organised a competition. The winners will receive one of these prizes.

Here are some of the people who entered the competition:

- A man who likes an adventurous life
- Two students
- A retired married couple
- A woman with a very difficult job

a 🎧 Listen to these two people. Tick (✓) which winner(s) they're talking about.

b 🎧 Listen again and look back to the **Useful Language** box in exercise 3. Tick (✓) the sentences if you hear them.

In pairs, decide what would be the best prize for the other people if they won. Use the language from the box.

Talking about 'needs'

5 Your discussion might also be about whether an object or an activity is *necessary* for a person. 🎧 Listen to what the examiner says:

In pairs, talk together about all the things, and then decide which four he should leave at home.

He might need … because

He definitely needs to take … because

He doesn't need … because

I (don't) think he needs … because

I (don't) think he should take … because

6 And you? Imagine you're getting ready for a one-week visit to a friend who lives in a foreign country. Make a list of the things to take with you (or not). Compare your list with a partner.

I definitely need	I want to take	I think I might need	I don't think I need

→ **See page 100 for Supplementary Activities.**

Speaking

UNIT 3 Discussing a situation (2)

In the exam

In Part 2 of the Speaking Test, the examiner gives you a visual to look at and describes a situation. You discuss it with your partner and decide what to do. You have about two to three minutes.

In this unit

- Getting started
- Getting your partner to join in
- Putting it all together
- Exam practice for Part 2

To start you thinking … about speaking for a minute

1 In the Speaking Test you don't have much time to think before speaking. So here's an idea to get you talking.

In pairs, write down as many nouns beginning with the letter M as you can think of in two minutes. (e.g. money, memory …)
Choose one of your words. Student A, talk about this word for one minute. Say *anything* about the topic – your feelings, some facts, etc. Student B, don't say anything. Time your partner and tell her/him to stop after one minute.
Choose another word and Student B, speak for one minute on that topic.

Getting started

2 Imagine the examiner has described a situation to you and you have the picture sheet in front of you. How do you begin?

a 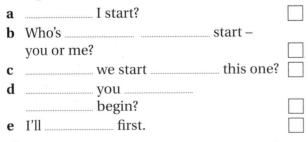 Listen and repeat these different ways of getting the discussion started.
Complete the sentences.

   a .... I start? ☐

   b Who's .... start – you or me? ☐

   c .... we start .... this one? ☐

   d .... you .... begin? ☐

   e I'll .... first. ☐

b Now listen to a short conversation. Tick (✓) any of the above phrases that you hear the two people using.

Getting your partner to join in

3 Imagine your partner is not saying very much about the choices on the picture sheet. Get her/him to speak by asking for opinions.

In pairs, decide how you could complete the questions below. Then listen and check your answers. Repeat each question with the recording.

> Useful language: giving and getting opinions
>
> a .... about this one?
> b .... you think .... this one?
> c What .... think we .... choose?
> d Why .... we choose a cheaper one?
> e I .... choose this one, don't you?
> f Do .... this is a good one?

4 In pairs, read the situations below.
Use some of the language from exercises 2 and 3
in your discussions.

Situation 1
You want to buy a present for a friend's birthday.
Discuss what's best.

Situation 2
Your school/college has a Students' Room. The
school/college wants to put one more thing in it
for the students. Discuss what's best.

Putting it all together

5 🎧 Listen and read these instructions.

I'm going to describe a situation to you. Your town has some money to spend on something new
for the area. Talk together about what you think would interest the people of the town and then
decide what new thing would be the most popular. Here is a picture with some ideas to help you.

🎧 Read a–c in the checklist below. Listen to two students discussing the task.
Tick (✓) the phrases you hear them using.

Checklist for Part 2

a How did the discussion begin?
Shall I start? ☐
You go first. ☐
Who's going to start? ☐

b Which of these ways of agreeing/disagreeing did you hear?
That's true. ☐
You're right. ☐
Yes, but ... ☐
I don't think so. ☐
I agree. ☐
I think so too. ☐

c What words did they use for their decision?
Let's go for ... ☐
What have we decided? ☐
We have to make a decision. ☐

🎧 Read d–g in the checklist. Listen to the discussion again and circle your answers.

d Were the examiner's instructions clear? — Yes/No
e Did each student ask the other one a question? — both did/one did /neither did
f Which student spoke most? — man/woman/equal
g How many of the ideas did they speak about? — 1 2 3 4 5 6

→ See page 101 for Supplementary Activities.

Exam practice for Part 2

🎧 Now it's your turn to try a complete Part 2. Listen
to the examiner's instructions.
Talk together for about three minutes. (see page 88)

Exam tip

- Look at your partner when you're speaking and also
  when you're listening
- Ask your partner for his/her ideas
- Remember to make a decision about what's best, most
  important, etc. at the end

Speaking

In the exam

In Part 3 of the Speaking Test, you are given a colour photograph and asked to talk about what's in the photo for about one minute.

In this unit

- Saying where something is in a photo
- Talking about the action in a photo
- Describing the people
- I don't know what it's called

To start you thinking ... about prepositions of place

1 **Where are the footballs? Write the correct letter on each ball.**

a above the goal	**f** in front of the goal
b on the right of the goal	**g** next to the coach
c in the middle of the goal	**h** behind the coach
d on a player's head	**i** in the corner of the goal
e between two players	**j** under a player

Saying where something is in a photo

2 **When you're talking about a picture you often need to say where something is.**
In pairs, you've both got a drawing of the same room but with different objects in it.
Student A: Look at this picture of a sitting room.
Student B: Turn to page 103 for your picture.
Student A: Your partner is going to ask you where some objects are in this room. Tell him/her.
Then you're going to ask her/him where the following objects are in his/her picture:

bookcase, picture, rug, magazines
clock, vase.

Complete the following sentences with the information you are given.

a There is a bookcase ....
b There's a picture ....
c The rug is ....
d There are some magazines ....
e The clock is ....
f There's a vase ....

Talking about the action in a photo

3 When you're talking about the different activities that are happening in your photo, use the present continuous:

e.g. There's a woman (and she's) sitting on the sofa.
I can see a boy (and he's) playing the piano.

(See Grammar File page 104.)

Look at the two photos on page 89. In pairs, take it in turns to be speaker and listener.
Student A: Tell your partner what's happening in Photo A.
Student B: Listen to your partner and circle the number of times (s)he uses the present continuous.   1   2   3   4   5   6   7   more
Then change roles for Photo B.

Describing people

4 Usually there will be a person or people in your photo. You will need to say what they're doing or say something about their appearance.

Choose the correct word (only one is possible).

a	They've both got blond	eyes/hair
b	He's got very pale	hair/skin
c	Her shoes .... expensive.	are/look
d	His hair .... long and curly.	is/looks
e	He's wearing really nice	dress/clothes
f	He's probably about 20	years old/years
g	He's quite	fat/thick
h	She's about 1.50 – that's really	short/low
i	He's very .... -looking.	well/good

🎧 **Look at these six people. Listen and tick (✓) which two people are being described.**

In pairs, take it in turns to talk about another person in the pictures. The listener should tick (✓) the person they think is being described. Use some of these ideas:

- (s)he's quite old, very tall, etc.
- (s)he's got dark hair, big eyes, a book in his hand, etc.
- (s)he's wearing smart clothes, jeans, sunglasses, etc.

Begin: In this picture I can see … or In this picture there's a …

I don't know what it's called

5 Imagine you're talking about your photo and you don't know the English word for something, what can you do?

- if it's not important, don't talk about it!
- if it *is* important, point to it and say that thing or I don't know what that's called
- or, try to talk about the object
  e.g. It's a thing for …-ing
      You can use it to …
      It's something you use when …

In pairs, imagine you don't know the English word for these objects. Choose one object and say one sentence like the example above. Your partner will point to the object you're describing.

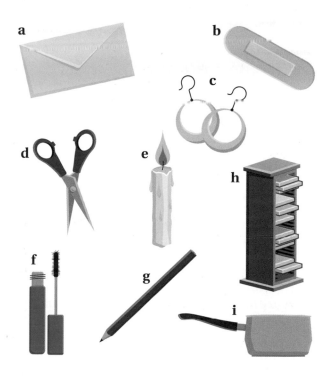

→ **See page 101 for Supplementary Activities.**

Speaking

UNIT 5 Talking about a picture (2)

In the exam

In Part 3 of the Speaking Test you are given a colour photograph and asked to talk about what's in the photo for about one minute.

In this unit

- Talking about impressions and opinions
- What to include
- Exam practice for Part 3

To start you thinking about … the word 'look'

1 Read this information about 'look'.

- *look* + adjective   e.g. He looks happy; It doesn't look very interesting.
- *look like* + noun   e.g. They don't look like sisters; It looks like a warm day.
- *look as if* + clause   e.g. It looks as if it's going to rain. (future possibility)
             She doesn't look as if she's enjoying the party. (talking about 'now')

Look at these pictures. Complete the sentences using the words in the box and the different *look* constructions above. There are two sentences for each photo.

summer
~~sad~~
hot
his father
she's going to cry
happy
empty
anyone is living there

a She _looks sad._   **c** It _____   **e** He _____   **g** It doesn't _____
b She _____   **d** It _____   **f** They don't _____   **h** It _____

In pairs, using the 'look' constructions, think of three sentences about different people in your class. Say your sentences to your partner. (S)he will guess who you are talking about.

e.g. *This person looks a bit bored at the moment.*

Talking about impressions and opinions

2 When you describe your picture, you can talk about facts (*The sky is blue*) or impressions (*It looks like summer*).
Here are some more ways of talking about your impressions and opinions:

- *might*   e.g. It **might be** someone's birthday (because …)
- *I think*   e.g. **I (don't) think** they're going on holiday (because …)
- *perhaps/maybe*   e.g. **Perhaps** she's tired (because …)
- *probably*   e.g. It's **probably** summertime (because …)

(see Grammar File page 110 for practice with these structures)

84

In pairs, talk about what these objects might be. Use the language on page 84 to say at least two things about each object.

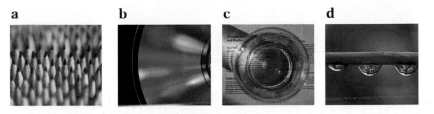
a   b   c   d

3 In pairs, look at the two photographs on page 89. Student A talk about photo A and Student B talk about photo B. Talk about your impressions and opinions of the people and the scenes.

When you're listening to your partner, tick if you hear any of the following:

look(s) ☐	looks as if ☐	maybe ☐	probably ☐
looks like ☐	I think ☐	might ☐	perhaps ☐

What to include

4 In the exam, try to include some different ideas. Look at the list below.
Work in pairs. Student A: Look at photo A on page 90 and answer Student B's questions.
Student B: Ask Student A the questions in the list below.

Place	Where is it? (e.g. *inside, in a town, in the countryside*)
Action	What are the people doing?
People	What are the people like? (e.g. *age, hair*)
	Who do you think the people are? (e.g. *friends, family*)
Clothes	What are they wearing?
Impression	How do they look? (e.g. *happy, worried*)
	What are they thinking / talking about?
	What's the place/scenery like? (e.g. *modern, beautiful*)
Ideas	What do you think is going to happen next?
Weather	Is there anything to say about the weather, or the time of year?
Other detail	Is there anything interesting in the rest of the picture?

Now, Student B: Look at photo B on page 90 and answer Student A's questions.
Student A: Ask student B the questions in the list above.

5 🎧 Listen to two students talking about the two photos on page 90.

Tick if the students:	Student A	Student B
a mention something about the place		
b talk about the appearance of the people		
c describe what's happening		
d give some impressions and opinions		
e give some other information		

f Which student do you think gives the better description?   A   B
g Suggest two things that might make the weaker description better. ....

➡ **See page 101 for Supplementary Activities.**

Exam practice for Part 3

Exam tip

- talk about fact and impressions
- practise talking about a photo for approximately one minute

In the Speaking Test you have about one minute to talk about your photo.

🎧 Student A: Look at photograph A on page 91 and then listen to the examiner telling you what to do.
Student B: Time Student A; tell him/her when one minute is finished.

Now change round. Student B: Look at photograph B on page 91. Student A: Time him/her.

Speaking

In the exam

In Part 4 of the Speaking Test you'll have a discussion with your partner on the topic of the photos from Part 3. You'll probably talk about your likes, dislikes and preferences, your habits and experiences, etc.

In this unit

- Questions to keep the conversation going
- Talking about your likes and dislikes
- Exam practice for Part 4

To start you thinking … about asking questions

1   Look at this questionnaire. It has been answered by Irish rock guitarist, Damien Childs, who is in Italy on a concert tour.
    In pairs, read his answers and then complete the questions.

Your questions will use different structures:
- present simple & continuous   e.g. Do you like …? What are you doing …?
- past   e.g. When did you go …?
- present perfect   e.g. How long have you been …?
- 'going to'   e.g. Are you going to …?
- would … like   e.g. Would you like to …?

a	Where …?	I've got a house in Dublin and an apartment in LA.
b	Do you …?	It's the best job in the world.
c	When …?	I've always played from when I was a child
d	What …?	I don't have much free time but I enjoy cooking for friends and dancing.
e	What kind …?	Everything from hip hop to jazz.
f	Who …?	At the moment, I'm listening to a lot of Jimi Hendrix.
g	Do you …?	Not much, no because people recognise me in the street. I use the Internet to buy a lot of things.
h	How long …?	A week – we've got gigs in Rome, Milan and Naples.
i	What …?	Well, I've only been here since Sunday but I love it – the food, the people, the sunshine.
j	Have …?	No, believe it or not, this is my first time here.
k	What would …?	Well, I don't really think about the future that much. Loads of people say they'd like to go into the movies but me, well I'll be happy just doing more of the same – making music.

Questions to keep the conversation going

2   After both of you have described the photos (see page 90), the examiner says:

Your photographs showed people listening to music. I'd like you to talk together about what kind of music you enjoyed when you were younger and what you like now.

To keep the discussion going, it's a good idea to ask your partner a question sometimes.

Can?   Do?   What?   Have?

What questions could you ask your partner?

Student A: Use these ideas to ask questions.

Student B: Answer the questions.

When?

a   What kind / enjoy?

b   When you were younger did …?

c   Who / favourite band or singer now?   Who?

d   Who / favourite / when / younger?

e   How often / listen /music?   Are?

f   like / go / concerts?

g   play / instrument?   How often?

After both of you have described the photos (see page 91), the examiner says:

> Your photographs showed food. I'd like you to talk together about the food you eat at home and the food you eat in restaurants.

Student B: Use these ideas to ask questions.

Student A: Answer the questions.

a   What kind / food / eat / home?

b   Do / enjoy / restaurants?

c   What / favourite food?

d   anything / not like?

e   How often / go / restaurant?

f   What / usually eat / lunchtime?

g   What / have / dinner/ last night?

h   Can / cook?

Talking about your likes and dislikes

3   **Decide what you think about these things: Put a tick (✓)under 🙂 , 😐 or ☹ .**

Subject	🙂	😐	☹
Watching football			
Dancing			
Flying			
Eating outside			
Lying on the beach			
Surfing the net			
Chatting with friends			
Watching videos			
Rain			
Shopping			

Look at the phrases in the box:

> really like   quite like   can't stand   don't mind
> am not very keen on   love   don't like … much

In pairs, take it in turns to tell your partner about one of the things you like or one of the things you don't like. If possible, say why.

e.g. I don't like lying on the beach much because it's boring.

Then ask your partner a question:

e.g. What about you?

or   What do you think about lying on the beach?

or   Do you like lying on the beach?

Repeat this four or five times.

Then talk to some more students in your class and see who you have the most in common with.

➡ **See page 101 for Supplementary Activities.**

Exam practice for Part 4

Exam tip

- the examiner says "talk together about …" That means you should ask each other questions, not just give your own opinions
- turn towards your partner so it's easier to talk together

🎧 **In this part of the exam, you'll have a discussion with your partner on the topic of the photos from Part 3.**

Turn to page 89 and look at the second pair of photos. Listen to the examiner's instructions.

Talk together. Allow about three minutes for this discussion.

When you've finished, check. Did you …

- both ask each other questions?   Yes / No
- use some different ways of saying *I like / I don't like*?   Yes / No
- say why you like going to certain places for holidays?   Yes / No
- talk about your ideas for future holiday places?   Yes / No

Speaking Unit 3, Exam practice

Speaking Unit 4, Exercise 3

Photo A Student A

Photo B Student B

Speaking Unit 5, Exercise 3; Speaking Unit 6, Exam practice

Photo A Student A

Photo B Student B

Speaking Unit 5, Exercise 4; Speaking Unit 6, Exercise 2

Photo A Student A

Photo B Student B

Speaking Unit 5, Exam practice; Speaking Unit 6, Exercise 2

Photo A Student A

Photo B Student B

Supplementary Activities

READING

Unit 1

1 Look at these signs. Where might you see them? What do they mean? Write your own ideas (there are no right or wrong answers!).

a .... b .... c .... d ....

e .... f .... g ....

2 Put the words into the correct order to make a notice or a label.

a this in Store position upright bottle an

....

b used building CCTV cameras are this in

....

c reception to report visitors All must

....

d keep with Passengers all them should luggage times at their

....

Unit 2

In Unit 2, page 8, there were lots of notices on a college notice board. Write one of your own to add to the notice board: either a notice about something you'd like to sell, or a message to leave for a friend about the volleyball practice tonight.

Unit 3

Word search. Find these words connected with *getting married.*

| groom   ring   honeymoon   marriage   reception |
| ceremony   engaged   fiance   guests   wedding |

You can move → ← ↑ ↓ ↖ ↗

N	O	O	M	Y	E	N	O	H
O	E	D	I	R	B	D	G	G
I	T	N	E	G	E	L	U	N
T	L	S	N	G	A	N	E	I
P	F	I	A	N	C	E	S	D
E	R	G	R	O	O	M	T	D
C	N	D	S	T	T	U	S	E
E	G	A	I	R	R	A	M	W
R	Y	N	O	M	E	R	E	C

Unit 4

Look back to the information about the five friends in exercise 1 on page 14. Who are these postcards from and who are they to?

a

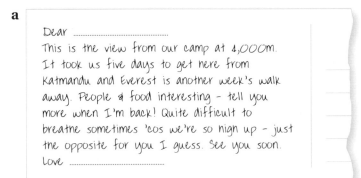

Dear ....
This is the view from our camp at 4,000m. It took us five days to get here from Katmandu and Everest is another week's walk away. People & food interesting – tell you more when I'm back! Quite difficult to breathe sometimes 'cos we're so high up – just the opposite for you I guess. See you soon.
Love ....

b

Dear ....
I'm really loving this holiday in Japan – our tour leader knows all the right places to take us, and if you show real interest in a particular dish, they'll even tell you how to make it. Looking forward to trying out some new ideas on you when we're both back – if I can persuade you to leave your desk for an hour or two!
Love ....

c

> Dear ....
> Yesterday I went fishing in the Red Sea with
> spearguns and then in the evening we had a BBQ
> on the beach. Fantastic - I now understand why you
> always said that nothing tastes better than fresh
> fish simply cooked - I agree! Today it was back
> to the serious stuff - we went down really deep
> and explored the wreck of a 19th century ship.
> Love ....

d

> Dear ....
> OK, so you're right about camping. We've just
> had a week of it out in the bush and it was
> great. At night we could lie there listening to
> the sounds of animals - we even had a friendly
> visit from a lion. I've seen everything I wanted
> to - except a cheetah but there's still time.
> Love ....

Unit 5

1 Read this text and the three statements which
follow. Decide which statement is *true* and which
two are *false*.

Return of the Cat

This is the story of Skittles, the ginger cat. His owner, Charmin
Sampson, was working temporarily in a summer camp in
Wisconsin, USA and had taken Skittles with her. When her job
came to an end and it was time to go back home, she
couldn't find the cat. After a day's search, she reluctantly left
him and drove home to Northern Minnesota. One morning,
five months later, she opened the front door to find a thin and
dirty Skittles outside. The cat had walked 350 miles across
two states, risked his life on the highway and survived
temperatures as low as -22 degrees.

a Charmin Sampson lived in Wisconsin.   T   F
b Before she left the camp, Charmin
tried very hard to find Skittles.   T   F
c Skittles had an accident on the highway.   T   F

Underline the mis-match in the false statements.

2 Imagine you want to enter the 'Experience Africa'
competition on page 19. Complete the sentence on
the competition form in not more than 15 words.

I would like to join the safari in Phinda because
....
....
....

Unit 6

Here are some statements about food and drink.
Decide whether you think these statements are *true*
or *false*. (You can do this in pairs.)

1 Eating cheese late in the evening will
give you bad dreams.   **T   F**
2 When you peel an onion, you'll cry unless
you use a wet knife.   **T   F**
3 Chewing gum was invented in the USA.   **T   F**
4 Carrots help you to see in the dark.   **T   F**
5 Fish is good for the brain.   **T   F**
6 If you're trying to cut down on fat,
eat earthworms.   **T   F**

Now read on to find the answers. The information is
not given in the same order.

a True. Research has shown that if you eat this, or
seafood, at least once a week, your mind has a
better chance of staying more active in old age.
b True. It may be OK for mice but it's not a good
idea for humans. There's something in it that
makes people have a bad night.
c False. But if you hold them under running water
to take the skins off, you'll be OK.
d True. These unattractive creatures are 72% protein
and less than 1% fat. And did you know that a
locust has more protein than a steak?
e True. Eyes need Vitamin A and the most
important source of Vitamin A is carotine which
was first found in this vegetable in 1831.
f False. In the 1st century AD, Greeks and Mayans
chewed a part of a special tree (the mastic tree) in
order to make their breath sweeter. The USA,
however, did begin the production of modern
chewing gum in the late 1860s.

Unit 7

1 Imagine you're going to interview Maisie
McNeice. Write two or three questions you would
like to ask her.

2 Maisie's story continues. Read it and then answer
the questions.

> People always ask me if I miss my friends and family in
> England, I do, but I keep in touch with them by email,
> and I love getting news from them. When I visit the UK
> I do notice I'm not as into fashion and make-up as my
> girlfriends. Sometimes in Botswana I miss cold weather,
> but I'm glad I live in Africa. We have such a different life
> but I wouldn't exchange it for anything in the world.

Me and my brothers have even had the chance to write a book about our life, something I never would have done at home. We don't go to school, Mum tutors us at home and we finish by 11am because the heat makes it hard to concentrate. I spend the rest of the day working with lions. Take it from me – nothing beats walking around barefoot and being outside in the sunshine. I feel very lucky to live the way I do.

1 How does Maisie feel when she visits the UK?
  A old-fashioned, compared with her friends
  B too cold to enjoy her visit
  C happy that she doesn't go to school there
  D excited at seeing her family
2 What does Maisie wish for sometimes?
  A fashionable clothes
  B normal school
  C cold weather
  D news from England

Unit 8

Think back again to the time when you were 12. Answer these questions (talk together in small groups).

  a Did you get any pocket money? (How much?)
  b What was your favourite object?
  c What was your least favourite item of clothing?
  d What kind of jobs did you do around the house?
  e What were your feelings about your school?
  f What were your hobbies or interests?
  g How much time did you spend on the computer?
  h Who was the most important person in your life?
  i Who was the most famous international person at the time?

Would your answers be different today? If so, in what way?

Think of two more questions to ask someone in your class.

Unit 9

1 Imagine a student has completed a gap-fill exercise, but has chosen the wrong answers. Look at these ten sentences: nine of them are incorrect, one is correct. Correct the mistakes. There's only one mistake in each sentence (preposition, quantity word or choice of vocabulary).

  a The house of the future will clean itself, so you won't waste time making housework.
  b Our apartment is in the second floor of the building.
  c It costs much to buy a house.
  d The TV aerial is fixed to the fireplace on the roof.
  e We've got great views from both windows.
  f Every of the rooms are full of plants.
  g The dog knocked the glass down the table and it broke.
  h There's anything wrong with the video.
  i You normally roast a chicken on the oven.
  j The washing machine does the washing-up for you. It's great!

2 In two minutes, write down:
  • three things you can turn on/off in the house.
  • three things you can sit on in the house.
  • three things you can open/close in the house or garden.

Unit 10

1 Put the words in the right order to make three well-known sayings about money:
  a go makes the round Money world
  b are life things best in free The
  c it happiness Money buy helps doesn't but

2 More work on word + preposition (see Appendix 2 page 117).

Choose the correct preposition and then match the two halves of the sentences.
with   for   about   by   about   by   ~~for~~

1 Paul won first prize   for (f)
2 Bus fares have gone up   ....
3 I gave him the wrong change   ....
4 People often argue   ....
5 What did you pay   ....
6 I'm sorry   ....
7 She shared her big win   ....

  a losing your lottery ticket.
  b money.
  c that book?
  d her sister.
  e mistake.
  f ~~his new painting~~.
  g a large amount this year.

WRITING

Unit 1

Student A: Look at this page. Student B: Look at page 103 (Pairwork Activities).

Student A: Complete these three sentences using your own ideas.

a   Why don't we ....?   (What about ...?)
b   .... two years ago.   (for two years)
c   .... was stolen yesterday. (Somebody)

Write your three sentences on a piece of paper. Below each sentence, copy the words in brackets. Give your sentences to a partner. (S)he will read your sentences and then write different ones using the words in brackets.

Unit 2

Write three sentences comparing yourself with another person in your family.
Give your sentences to someone else in the class. (S)he will try and rewrite your sentences to say the same things but in a different way.

Unit 3

1   Practice with *must(n't); (don't) have/need to; ought to/should*
    (see Grammar File page 110)

Complete the sentences in A with an appropriate ending from B.

A
1   You don't have to do this exercise …
2   You mustn't be late for the meeting …
3   We all had to work late last night …
4   I think you should take a taxi …
5   You must get a letter from your doctor …
6   You ought to go and see it …
7   I don't think you should buy it …

B
a   because it's a good film.
b   if you want to get there early.
c   if you don't want to.
d   because it always starts on time.
e   because it's too expensive.
f   because there was a lot to do.
g   if you're absent for more than three days.

2   In pairs, write some 'rules' that friends should have between them:

You should/ought to …   You must …
You don't have/need to …   You mustn't …
You shouldn't …

Compare your rules with others in your class.

Unit 4

Look at these notes. Write them again as complete sentences (there is an example).

Example

Sally
Computer's crashed!
Gone to Internet Café.
Back before 7.

Sally, my computer's crashed so I've gone to the Internet Café. I'll be back before 7.00.

A

Tony
Change of plan. Meet at cinema, not café at 7.30.
Matt not coming.

B

Leo
Mohamed rang at 11.15. Ring him back a.s.a.p. – some interesting news!

C

Gina
Wonderful news about job!
Really happy for you.
Dinner next week?

Unit 5

1 **Look at these text messages. They're all about love. What are they saying?**

a WenCnICUAgn? = ...

b UdoSumthn2Me = ...

c UblwMyMnd = ...

2 **Read this question and the answer that follows. Then write the three points you were asked to include.**

You are on holiday, and are sending a postcard to a friend. Write your postcard in 35–45 words. In your postcard you should

- ....
- ....
- ....

Dear Sophie
Here I am in Scotland with my friend, Martin. We're having a walking holiday along the west coast and I'm really enjoying it. But the best thing is the weather – so far, 5 days of wonderful sunshine. See you soon.
Love

Unit 6

Here are eight sentences from two different letters.

Letter 1 – about keeping fit
Letter 2 – about learning Spanish

Which sentences belong to which letter? For each letter, find the first sentence, then the last sentence, then decide on the order for the two middle sentences.

a The other is that you mustn't be afraid of making mistakes.

b Anyway, keep on jogging – I'm looking forward to seeing a new, fit person when we next meet.

c Good to hear you've started learning Spanish – you asked me for some suggestions, so here are one or two.

d For me, the most important thing is to do regular exercise, even when you don't feel like it.

e Good luck with it all. Don't study too hard.

f Thanks for your letter – I'm happy to tell you how I try to keep fit.

g The first one is to use the language as much as you can.

h So that's what I do – every day at the same time, even when it's cold and wet.

Letter 1 sentence letters: ....
Letter 2 sentence letters: ....

Unit 7

Antonio is going to England to stay with his friend, Kevin, in Oxford. Unfortunately, Antonio spilt some coffee on Kevin's letter. Can you fill in the gaps? Sometimes you need to complete a word, sometimes you need to write one or more extra words.

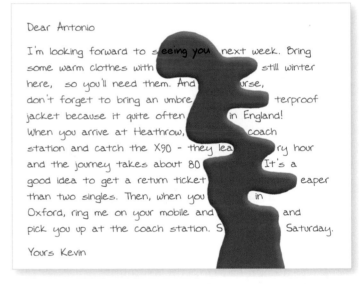

Dear Antonio

I'm looking forward to seeing you next week. Bring some warm clothes with .... still winter here, so you'll need them. And .... urse, don't forget to bring an umbre......... terproof jacket because it quite often .... in England! When you arrive at Heathrow, ... coach station and catch the X90 – they lea......... ry hour and the journey takes about 80 .... It's a good idea to get a return ticket .... eaper than two singles. Then, when you .... in Oxford, ring me on your mobile and .... and pick you up at the coach station. S......... Saturday.

Yours Kevin

Unit 8

1 **You and a friend are going on holiday to Ireland tomorrow. You've packed your suitcases but there are some more things to add. You can't take them all.**

In pairs, decide what
- you're definitely going to take
- you'd like to take
- you're thinking of taking
- you don't want to take
- you don't think you'll need
- you hope you'll be able to take

pair of scissors	CDs	laptop
favourite chocolate	mobile	books
address book	phrase book	hairdryer
swimming things		

2 This is part of a letter you receive from an English friend, Jack.

> *... and how did you spend your birthday? Tell me everything!*

Write a letter (about 100 words) using the notes in your diary to help you.

SATURDAY, FEBRUARY 14TH

Morning:	Weight training class – hard work Met Agnes in Blackwell's coffee shop
Afternoon:	Shopping – new trousers, but not sure about them now
Evening:	Cinema with Sam. 'Monsoon Wedding' – brilliant

> Dear Jack
> Thanks for your letter. My birthday was fun, but I didn't have a party this year. In the morning, I ....

Continue the letter; write about 100 words.

Unit 9

1 Choose a time, a person, a place and an object from below, and make up a short story (maximum three sentences) to include all four things. Tell your partner your story.

time	person	place	object
two years ago	doctor	bathroom	snake
last weekend	student	boat	lots of money
in 2001	actor	tent	letter
yesterday	musician	Rome	apple
last night	child	garden	computer

2 Look at this picture of Linda. Write a 100-word story about how she broke her arm. Begin "One day Linda was …" Use some different past tenses to describe what happened. If you need any help, the story "The day I broke my leg" on page 53 will help you.

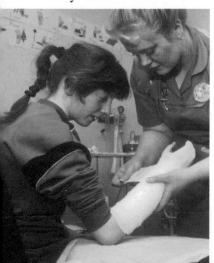

Unit 10

Practice with linkers.

and	but	so	because	although
fortunately	unfortunately	suddenly		

In pairs, imagine this was last week's weather:

Monday:	raining	Thursday:	foggy
Tuesday:	snowing	Friday:	windy
Wednesday:	very cold	Saturday:	warm and sunny

Student A: Choose one of the linkers above for Student B to use.
Student B: Say something about Monday's weather using Student A's linker.
Then change roles. e.g.

A: Suddenly
B: *I was sitting on the balcony and suddenly it began to rain.*

LISTENING

Unit 1

Think of some numbers that are important in your life, e.g. when you were born or how many CDs you've got. In pairs, dictate these numbers to each other and write them down. Try and guess why these numbers are important in your partner's life.

Unit 2

This is the tapescript of a Part 1 question. Read it, look at the question, and write a description of the three pictures (two incorrect, one correct) that you think should be there, or draw the pictures if you prefer.

Man on phone: I'm in the kitchen, getting dinner ready for Jane and her family – they're coming at seven. Trouble is I'm not a very good cook. I'm very good at making a mess – you should see the amount of washing-up I have when I cook. But to be honest, I don't really enjoy it. I get quite interested when I read cookbooks but actually doing it …

What's the man doing at the moment?

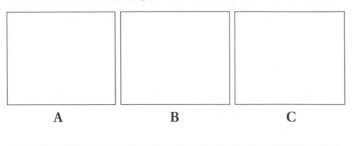

A   B   C

Unit 3

Look at sentences *a* to *l* in exercise 2 on page 62.
In pairs, take it in turns to say one of the sentences
in each pair, and see if your partner can decide
which one you are saying!

Unit 4

Work in pairs. Student A: Look at the Café picture
below. Student B: Look at the café picture on page
101. Don't look at each other's pictures. Talk
together and see if you can find seven differences.

Student A

Unit 5

Vocabulary for films and the cinema. Complete the
sentences. The first part of each word and the
number of letters are shown.

a What's o _ at the cinema this week?
b The di _ _ _ _ _ _ of the film is Baz Lahman and
   the main a_ _ _ _ is Ewan McGregor.

c You usually buy your tickets at the b _ _ o _ _ _ _ _.
d I don't want to sit at the back because I can't see
   the sc _ _ _ _ very well.
e The best sc _ _ _ in the film is where the man finds
   the letter.
f Nicole Kidman p _ _ _ _ the part of a dancer in the
   film.
g The film had a really sad en _ _ _ _ and everyone
   in the audience cried.
h What's your favourite kind of film – a c _ _ _ _ _
   that makes you laugh or an ac _ _ _ _ film like
   Indiana Jones or maybe a thr _ _ _ _ _ which is
   really exciting?

Unit 6

Spelling: how many different words can you find?
Find a word, spell it to your partner, he/she will
write it down. Try to find 20 between you.

Rules • words must be a minimum of three letters
      • you can take letters from anywhere in the
        grid
      • no plural words allowed.

G	A	S
L	M	E
O	T	I

Unit 7

1 Look at the information you filled in for Darius
  Gallagher on page 70.
  In pairs, talk together about whether you think
  he should be one of the 12 people chosen for the
  Survival Challenge. What are his strong points
  and his weak points?

2 Copy the application form (page 70) onto a piece
  of paper. Fill it in on behalf of a friend or family
  member (you can use your imagination if you
  like) but don't write the person's name. Put your
  form together with all the other forms from
  people in your class. In groups of three or four
  take some application forms and discuss who
  you think would be the best person for Survival
  Challenge.

Unit 8

1 Vocabulary for describing a person's character. Match the questions to the adjectives in the box.

relaxed	friendly	clever	shy
honest	cheerful	generous	funny

a Do you find it difficult to meet and talk to people?

b Are you happy and always have a smile on your face?

c Can you understand and learn things easily?

d Do you always tell the truth?

e Do you believe in taking life easy and not worrying about things?

f Do you make people laugh?

g Are you warm and open and like being with people?

h Do you pay for your friends when you go out?

2 How would you describe yourself? Tell your partner, using some of the adjectives:

I think I'm …   I don't think I'm …

3 These three adjectives have the opposite meaning to three in the box. Match them.

mean   stupid   sad

Unit 9

Look at the list of animals in the box below.
In pairs, decide how you can re-organise them into three different lists.

Rules • your lists must have titles (e.g. useful animals, *or* they all have legs)
       • you must place *all* the animals somewhere

camel	dog	rat	elephant	lion
shark	mosquito	kangaroo	wolf	bee
snake	eagle	cow	cat	monkey

List 1: ....   List 2: ....   List 3: ....

SPEAKING

Unit 1

Think of five questions that people who don't know you might ask you. Don't write the questions, write your answers.

e.g.   From Spain.
       No, I'm a student.
       Two brothers.

In pairs, say your answers to your partner, or someone else in your group. They will try and say the questions that you were thinking of.

Unit 2

Game: Match the Person to the Present

In pairs or small groups: choose a person and then choose a present. You must say why this person would like or need this present. Your partner(s) can agree or disagree with your choice (but must say why).

You can also play this game by photocopying the page and cutting up the squares to make cards. Deal out the People cards and put the Present cards face down on the table. Student 1 starts by putting a Person card on the table and picking up a Present card. You must say why this person would like or need the present. The first student to match all their people with presents is the winner.

People cards

Present cards

Unit 3

In pairs, discuss your answers to these questions about spending money.

a What do you spend most of your money on?

b What have you bought today?

c What was your last 'big' buy?

d Does it usually take you long to decide what to buy?

e Do you find it easy to choose presents for other people?

f Do you prefer shopping alone?

g What things do you think are expensive in your country?

h Do you think both men and women are interested in shopping?

Unit 4

Vocabulary: clothes and things you wear.
Think of something you wear (clothes, jewellery, etc) for these letters of the alphabet.

A for anorak	K for ....
B for	N for ....
C for	P for ....
D for	R for ....
E for	S for ....
F for	T for ....
G for	U for ....
H for	V for ....
J for	W for ....

Listening, Unit 4

Student B

Unit 5

In pairs, look at this picture of a market.
Student A: Give a fact about something or somebody in the picture.
Student B: Give your impression of something or somebody in the picture.
Then change roles. Say at least five sentences each.

Unit 6

1 Question practice: make correct questions by putting the words in the right order.

a go often to How cinema you the do?

b you Who out tonight going are with?

c car a long had have How you?

d university want do to you study Which at?

e always in been cooking you Have interested?

2 Fluency activity: 'That's a lie!'

- Think about all the things you did last night. Try and remember at least six different things. Then think of one thing you didn't do (you can make it something very ordinary).

- Tell your partner what you did last night; include your 'lie'. Begin:
  Last night I ...

- Your partner must try and guess the lie.

Pairwork Activities

READING

Unit 6 Exercise 3

Student B

Complete these four statements on *The Ups and Downs of 50 Years of Running* (page 21), using the words below.

If you see **F**, make the statement false.
If you see **T**, make the statement true.

disagreed   fast   before   difficult   record

a The New Zealander's weight made
it .... for him to run ....   **T**

b Running became popular in the
USA .... the Munich Olympics.   **F**

c In 1981, the first two men to complete
the London Marathon .... about
how to cross the finishing line.   **F**

d In 1987, a British woman set a new
.... in the New York Marathon.   **F**

Write these four complete statements (without **T/F**) on a piece of paper. Give it to your partner to decide if the statements are *true* or *false*.

Unit 8 Exercise 2

Student B: Read Debbie's story and make notes on the four questions that follow.

Debbie's story

When I was 12 ... in 1963

It was an exciting time – The Beatles had just hit the music scene and we were mad about them. And fashion was important for us – it seemed to change so quickly, suddenly miniskirts were everywhere. I got a bit of pocket money and I'm sure I spent it all on clothes.

My all-girls school wasn't great – we had one particularly useless subject called housecraft classes. They taught us how to lay tables and iron men's shirts. Even then I can remember thinking I don't want to spend my life doing this! I wanted to do woodwork

classes – but you could only do that at the boy's school. We had all just got record players and we used to borrow each other's records. My friend, Sheila, lost an Elvis record of mine – I've never forgiven her! I read quite a lot, but what we really wanted to do was go to the cinema – that was much more exciting because boys went there. We didn't go very often, unfortunately. As for my parents, they weren't really strict – I just had to keep my room tidy – my sister didn't even do that. She was really lazy. I remember my Mum got a new washing machine which she loved – she spent hours with that machine, especially at the weekends. We had the cleanest clothes in the town!

What does Debbie say about:
a clothes *fashion important;* ....
....
b school ....
c boy/girl relationships ....
d housework ....

Student B: Now answer the following multiple-choice questions on Debbie's story. (There's only one correct answer for each question.) Write your answers on a separate piece of paper.

e What is Debbie's main point about clothes?
  A People spent too much money on them.
  B They were very important for young people.
  C People didn't approve of miniskirts.
  D Fashions changed too quickly.

f What does Debbie say about her school?
  A She thinks it was useless.
  B She really enjoyed it.
  C She found one subject a waste of time.
  D She enjoyed the woodwork classes.

g What do we learn about boy/girl relationships?
  A Girls were very interested in meeting boys.
  B They met regularly at the cinema.
  C Girls wanted to learn useful things for when they got married.
  D They were not very interested in each other.

h What does the writer say about housework?
  A Her mother did it all.
  B She did a very small amount of it.
  C It was only done at weekends.
  D Her sister helped more than she did.

When you're ready, ask your partner what Kate said about the four topics, a–d above.

WRITING

Unit 1 Supplementary Activities

Student B: Complete these three sentences using your own ideas.

a .... belong to?   (Whose ...?)
b .... for three years.   (It's three years)
c .... is not far from yours.   (quite near)

Write your three sentences on a piece of paper. Below each sentence, copy the words in brackets. Give your sentences to a partner. (S)he will read your sentences and then write different ones using the words in brackets.

LISTENING

Unit 6 Exercise 3

Student B: Listen to your voicemail message from your partner. Write it down.

Now, it's your turn to ring your partner's voicemail and leave a message.

• give your name
• tell her/him you're back from your holidays (where did you go?) and would like to meet
• ask her/him to ring you back

Your partner will write down your message.

SPEAKING

Unit 1 Exercise 2

Student B: Complete the sentences in Set 1 and Set 2 with *one* word.

Student B: Set 1
a IT is short for _ _ _ _ _ _ _ _ _ _ technology.
b The opposite of 'full' is _ _ _ _ _ .
c How much did your new mobile _ _ _ _ ?

d The hospital took an _-_ _ _ of my leg to see if it was broken.
e A _ _ _ _ _ _ _ is another word for an 'error'.
f The Pacific is the biggest _ _ _ _ _ in the world.

Student B: Set 2
a The capital of Portugal is _ _ _ _ _ _ .
b The floor was _ _ _ _ _ so I washed it.
c During the week I have to get up _ _ _ _ _ but at the weekends I get up much later.
d My brother has a daughter, which means that she is my _ _ _ _ _ .
e The armed forces consist of the army, the _ _ _ _ and the airforce.
f Wine is made from _ _ _ _ _ _ .
g 'Z' is the last letter in the English _ _ _ _ _ _ _ _ .

Unit 4 Exercise 2

Student B: Look at this picture of a sitting room.

Ask Student A where the following objects are in his/her picture:

sofa, lamp, TV, videos, the remote control.

Complete the following sentences with the information you are given.

a The sofa is ....
b There's a lamp ....
c The TV is ....
d The videos are ....
e The remote control is ....

Now your partner will ask you where some objects are in this room. Tell him/her.

Grammar File

Use the present simple
- to describe what someone regularly or always does (*He works in a bank.*)
- for general facts (*The sun sets in the west.*)

Use the present continuous
- to describe what's happening now, at this time (*I'm watching TV.*)

e.g. *In the photograph, you can see a café. A man is sitting at a table with a woman but they aren't talking to each other. They come here every day. He usually drinks coffee but today they're both having some wine. She doesn't like coffee.*

Watch out!

There are some verbs which are not used in the continuous form. The most common are:

like	want	know
dislike	wish	prefer
love	hate	understand

Exercise 1

Present simple or present continuous? Choose the right verb form to complete the sentences.

Dear Ricky
Here's a picture of me and Miguel on holiday! We **(1)** *stay / are staying* on a small island which not many people **(2)** *know / are knowing* about. In fact, we are almost the only tourists here, so we **(3)** *don't want / are not wanting* too many others to discover our secret place!
Our daily life is very pleasant. Every morning, we **(4)** *get / are getting* up between 9 and 10, and **(5)** *have / are having* a long, relaxed breakfast – just as **(6)** *I do / am doing* now, which is probably why this letter's got butter on it – sorry! After breakfast we **(7)** *spend / are spending* about ten seconds making the big decision about where to spend the day, and of course we **(8)** *always go / are always going* to the beach.
Anyway, how are you? I hope you **(9)** *get / are getting* on all right in your new job, and that you **(10)** *don't work / aren't working* too hard.
See you in a couple of weeks
Lots of love Nina

Use the past simple
- to describe things that happened at a definite time in the past (*I started my new job in April 2002.*)

Use the past continuous
- to give some 'background' to your past description (*Dave woke up and looked out of the window yesterday morning. The sun was shining and the birds were singing.*)

yesterday

- to add 'drama' to a story (*I was walking home last night when suddenly something fell on my head.*)

(last night)

Exercise 2

Past simple or past continuous? Choose the correct form of the verb.

Kenji **(1)** *ate / was eating* his breakfast when suddenly he **(2)** *heard / was hearing* a loud noise from outside. It **(3)** *sounded / was sounding* like a firework.

He **(4)** *ran / was running* to the window, and **(5)** *looked / was looking* out. He could see a lot of people in the street; some of them **(6)** *shouted / were shouting* and some of them **(7)** *laughed / were laughing*.

Then suddenly Kenji **(8)** *understood / was understanding* what **(9)** *happened / was happening*.

The people **(10)** *waited / were waiting* to see their football team, Manchester United, who were coming through the city to show everyone their championship cup.

PAST SIMPLE and PAST PERFECT

Use the past simple
- to describe things that happened at a definite known time in the past (*When did you learn to snowboard? Last year, in France.*)
- to tell stories (*Once there was an old man who lived in a castle.*)

Use the past perfect
- when you're describing a past event using the past simple, and you want to show a connection between that event and an earlier one. (*When I arrived, everybody had already left.*)

6:00 pm   6:30 pm   (now) 10:00 pm

Exercise 3

Complete the sentences using the past simple or past perfect.

a Mario opened the door. A woman was standing there. He __had never seen__ (*never / see*) her before in his life.

b Many people believe that Columbus _____ (*discover*) America in the year 1492.

c Before I lived in Japan, I _____ (*never / eat*) raw fish.

d When we woke up it was raining, but by the time we left the house the rain _____ (*stop*).

e Everybody in the class _____ (*relax*) as soon as the inspector left the room.

f Simon thought his computer was broken, until his little brother pointed out that he _____ (*forget*) to switch it on.

g Philosophers in the Middle Ages thought it _____ (*be*) possible to turn metal into gold.

PRESENT PERFECT (1) FOR / SINCE

Use the present perfect
- to show a connection between past and present

PAST
I met Ulrica in 1974.

PRESENT PERFECT
I have known her for 30 years.

PRESENT
We are still good friends.

Use *for* before a period of time:
for 30 years, for 3 days, for ages

PAST ←… FOR THREE DAYS→ NOW

Use *since* before a point in time:
since yesterday, since 1999, since my birthday

PAST … SINCE YESTERDAY NOW

Exercise 4

Write *for* or *since*.

a That cat has been on the wall ____since____ this morning.

b Carole saw Sam on Wednesday but nobody has spoken to him _____ then.

c Bill Gates has been head of Microsoft _____ more than twenty years.

d Have you seen him _____ the party?

e He's lived on a boat _____ he got married.

f _____ last year, Katya has changed jobs three times.

g Juan hasn't been to work _____ five days.

h Sorry I'm late. Have you been waiting here _____ ages?

PRESENT PERFECT (2)

Use the present perfect
- for 'indefinite past' situations – you don't know 'when', or 'when' is not important
  "Is John there?" "No, sorry, he's gone out."

The present perfect is really about the present – we're not interested in **when** John went out, but in the fact that he isn't here **now**.

- with *ever, never, just, already, yet*

A: *Have you ever visited China?*
B: *Yes, I've been there several times.*
A: *Have things changed much since your first visit?*
B: *Yes, there have been big changes.*

Exercise 5

Use the correct form of the present perfect to complete the sentences with a verb from the box.

~~see~~	go	lose	buy
decide	finish	hear	play

a   *Has* anyone here *seen* *Lord of the Rings*?
b   We _____n't _____ where to go for our holidays yet.
c   _____ the team manager ever _____ any really good players?
d   Dieter _____n't _____ repairing the car yet.
e   Matti's not very happy – he just _____ a lot of money.
f   We _____ never _____ of the group who are playing tonight.
g   _____ you _____ any good games on your computer recently?
h   It's only three o'clock, but several staff _____ already _____ home.

PAST SIMPLE and PRESENT PERFECT

Use the past tense
• for completed/finished actions, if we know when they happened
   (*I left college three years ago.*)

Use the present perfect
• when something began in the past, but is still true (*I've known her for 30 years.*)
• if the time when something happened is not known, or is not important (see Present perfect (2)) (*I've visited China several times.*)

e.g. Marc: *I've lost my keys!*
      Gina: *No, you haven't. They're here in my pocket. You gave them to me last night, when we came home.*

Exercise 6

Are the underlined words right or wrong? Correct them if they're wrong.

a   When <u>have you bought</u> that hat?
      Wrong. When did you buy that hat?
b   I <u>never went</u> to Russia, but I'd like to.

c   Mika <u>has met</u> an old friend yesterday – someone he <u>went</u> to school with.

d   Very few people <u>have heard</u> of Alexis Kivi, but he's my favourite writer.

e   I'm really hungry – I <u>didn't eat</u> anything since last night.

f   <u>Have you seen</u> the fantastic firework display last night? Definitely the best <u>I saw</u> since I came here.

PASSIVE with past simple and present simple

Active sentences begin with the person who does or did something (the subject).
past simple
      Shah Jahan   built   the Taj Mahal.
         He   →   built   →   it.
      (subject) + past of 'to build' + object

present simple
Thousands of tourists visit the Taj Mahal every day.
      They   →   visit   →   it.

Passive sentences begin with the object.
past simple
      The Taj Mahal was built by Shah Jahan.
         It   ←   was built   ←   by him.
present simple
The Taj Mahal is visited by thousands of tourists.
         It   ←   is visited   ←   by them
The passive verb form is:

the verb 'to be'   +   past participle
was / were   +   *built; taken*
is / are   +   *told; made*

Exercise 7

Complete the passive sentences a–g below by adding the correct form of the verb 'to be' – past or present, singular or plural. Choose from *is, are, was, were,* or (rarely) *am.*

a The World __was__ first circumnavigated in 1522.

b A lot of the clothes which _____ sold in Europe nowadays _____ made in the Far East.

c At every Olympics, at least one world record _____ always broken.

d The star said: "I can't go shopping like other people, because I _____ always stopped in the street and asked for autographs."

e The house where I live _____ built in 1936.

f I prefer films which _____ shown in their original language.

g Fireworks _____ invented by the Chinese several hundred years ago.

Sentences h and i are similar to sentences b and c, but now active, not passive. Fill in the verbs, in the correct form.

h Factories in the Far East _____ a lot of the clothes which shops in Europe now _____ .

i At every Olympics, at least one athlete always _____ a world record.

WILL and GOING TO

Use will
* to talk about the future with

I hope I'll …	I don't know if I'll …
I expect he'll …	I'm sure you'll …
I (don't) think it'll …	I'll probably …

It's late. I don't think he'll come now.
I expect he'll stay at the hotel and come tomorrow.

Use going to
* to talk about your intentions or plans

I'm not going to eat anything today, because I'm on a diet.

Exercise 8

Write down five things that you intend to do, or not to do, this month. Use *going to* or *not going to*
e.g. I'm going to stay with my cousin. I'm not going to work too hard.

a _____

b _____

c _____

d _____

e _____

And what are the chances of these things happening to your family and friends? Use *I hope he'll, I expect she'll, I (don't) think he'll, I'm sure they'll, I don't know if we'll, She'll probably.*)

e.g. *John will probably go to college to study.*

f learn another language _____

g live abroad _____

h meet the perfect partner _____

i learn to drive _____

j get a new job _____

k become famous _____

PRESENT CONTINUOUS with future meaning

Use the present continuous for the future
* when something is fixed, you have already arranged to do it (It is written in your diary or you have got the tickets in your pocket).
I can't come at 11 o'clock tomorrow. I'm teaching Class 9.

Exercise 9

Write complete sentences using the present continuous. All the sentences are in the 'already arranged' future.

a you / do / anything tonight?
   Are you doing anything tonight?

b What / you / do / for your summer holidays this year?
   _____

c What time / Paul / meet us?
   _____

d Sonia can't come to the cinema because she / babysit / tonight.
   _____

e Zoe / have / a party on Saturday for her birthday.
   _____

f Our next-door neighbours / move / next month.
   _____

g How many people / come / to dinner tonight?
   _____

h you / work / at the weekend?
   _____

LINKING WORDS (1) because, but, although, so

Use because
- to give the reason why something happened
  I stayed at home this morning ← → because I felt ill.

Use but
- to introduce something which is the 'opposite' of the first sentence
  It was difficult to learn, but we enjoyed it.
  (− → +)

Use although/though
- to introduce an opposite
  Although Anna was tired, she stayed until the end of the party. (− → +)
  The restaurant was really nice, though we didn't enjoy the meal. (+ → −)

Use so
- to introduce an action which follows as a result of another action
  The door was open, so (→) I went in.

Exercise 10

Complete the sentences in your own words.

a Jane gave me a new sweater yesterday, but
   I don't like it .
b I usually walk to college but _____
c Although _____ , David bought it.
d It was hot in the room so _____
e Ben didn't win the tennis match, although
   _____
f I wouldn't like to live in a small village, because
   _____
g Miro is quite a small man, but _____
h There was nobody interesting at the party, so
   _____
i It was a bright sunny day, so _____
j Because Jaime was feeling so happy,
   _____

LINKING WORDS (2) as soon as, after, before, until, when, while

- as soon as and when have a similar meaning, but as soon as is more precise; when is very general
  When everybody was there, the meeting began.
  David bought the CD as soon as it appeared in the shops.

  You can put these linkers at the beginning or in the middle of the sentence.

- before and after join two actions – first one action, then another
  I shut all the windows before I left the house.
  (1st action: shut, 2nd action: left)
  After Jo had finished lunch, she started work.
  (1st action: finished, 2nd action: started work)

- until means up to a certain time, but not after it.
  I usually stay at the office until 8 o'clock or until I finish all my work.

- while (often with a continuous tense) joins two actions happening at the same time
  While I was living in Japan, I learnt karate.
  I like listening to music while I'm working.

Exercise 11

Complete each sentence using one of the six linkers above. There is usually more than one possible answer.

a Please don't talk to me __while (when)__ I'm trying to work.
b _____ Marushka entered the room, she knew that something was wrong.
c The President will make his speech _____ he has opened the museum.
d It's difficult to talk to the dentist _____ he's got his fingers in your mouth.
e You can't take the computer home _____ you've paid for it.
f Marek knew that the house would feel empty _____ Ewa left home.
g We sometimes have to wait _____ almost 9 o'clock for the 8 o'clock bus.
h Wait _____ the engine is cooler _____ you check the oil and water.
i _____ our grandparents have had lunch, they always fall asleep.
j Tina turned off the computer _____ she went to bed.

COMPARISON

When you compare things using adjectives, check how many syllables the adjectives have.

- one syllable words and two syllable words which end in –y
  → *(a bit/much) older than /happier than*

- longer words (two or more syllables)
  → *(a lot/much) more expensive than*

- negative comparison
  → *not as expensive as/not as many as*

Superlative forms:

- short words → *the oldest* (*in the world*)
- long words → *the most exciting …* (*I've ever seen*)

e.g. *Jacques, Marc and Michel are brothers. Jacques is 18, Marc is 16, and Michel is 14. Marc is older than Michel. Jacques is the oldest of the three.*

Computers aren't as expensive as they used to be, and the software is much cheaper than it was. My computer is the best thing I've ever bought – I couldn't live without it.

Watch out!

good/ well	better than	the best
bad	worse than	the worst
little	less than	the least

Exercise 12

Only one of these sentences is correct. Correct the mistakes where necessary.

a Which is the more bigger city in the world?

b Michel is not as older than Marc.

c It's much more difficult to snowboard than I expected.

d My brother is a more good skier than me.

e There seems to be little snow in winter as there used to be.

f Winters are more warm than they were.

g It was one of the difficultest decisions I've ever made.

h Many people think that Prague is the more beautiful as Paris.

Complete these three sentences comparing yourself now with yourself five years ago.

i I'm not ....

j I used to be ....

k I'm a bit ....

VERBS + to … VERBS +…-ing

When one verb follows another in a sentence, the second verb is either in the infinitive or an –ing form.

I've decided to leave college.
What do you enjoy doing at the weekend?

Common verbs followed by infinitive	Common verbs followed by -ing
want	spend (time/money)
hope	enjoy
decide	like
try	love
learn	stop
forget	finish
plan	look forward to *

Prepositions are followed by the –ing form

Thank you for listening to me.
I'm looking forward to seeing you soon.
(* *to* is a preposition and part of the phrase *look forward*)

Watch out!

Do you like reading books?	BUT	**Would** you **like to** see it?
I love swimming.		I**'d love to** travel.
I prefer getting up early.		I**'d prefer to** leave college.

Exercise 13

Put the verb in the right form: use *to …* or *-ing*.

Dear Amanda

Did I tell you I'm learning **(1)** __to drive__ (drive)? I think it'll be useful because I'm going to spend a month **(2)** .... (travel) round Italy in the summer. Daniela and I have decided **(3)** .... (go) together. Would you like **(4)** .... (join) us? It'll be fun.

We both finish **(5)** .... (study) at the end of June and we hope **(6)** .... (start) our holiday in the first week of July. We're planning **(7)** .... (camp) because it's cheaper and it'll be warm in July. And I really love **(8)** .... (sleep) outside.

By the way, I forgot **(9)** .... (tell) you, Daniela's getting married in September so she wants **(10)** .... (enjoy) her last holiday with her women friends!

Let me know if you're interested in **(11)** .... (come) with us.

Looking forward to **(12)** .... (hear) from you soon.

Love Gaby

POSSIBILITY

definitely   probably   might   perhaps/maybe
100% sure   ←←   It's possible   →→   Don't know

Someone asks: *Where's Jason? He's not answering the door.* Look at these different answers.

Nick: He might be in his room. He might not be able to hear you.
Roberto: He's definitely out with Mario.
Sasha: He's probably talking to his girlfriend.
Pedro: Perhaps he's gone to the café.

Exercise 14

Look at the pictures and answer the questions. Use the words above to show how sure you are.

1

2

a   Where do you think this is?
b   What time of year is it?
c   What's the relationship between the people?
d   What are they talking about?

OBLIGATION

must ← ought to/ ⎫ ← → ⎧ don't have/ → must not
         should   ⎭   ⎩ need to

Must means that the regulations say it is 100% necessary to do this.
must not means that it is 100% forbidden.

You must wait for the green light before you cross the road.
You must not cross while the light is red.

Ought to and should mean that it is a good idea to do this.

You ought to speak to Dr Foster – he'll tell you what to do.
You should say 'yes' to the offer – you can change your mind later.

Don't have to and don't need to mean that it is not necessary – you can decide whether to do it or not.

You don't have to finish the potatoes if you've had enough.
We don't need to finish the report until Monday.

Watch out!

'should do it', but 'ought **to** do it'

Exercise 15

Complete each sentence with one of the phrases above.

a   When you're at sea, you ___must___ do exactly what the ship's captain tells you to do.
b   You _____ listen to what experienced sailors say – you can learn a lot from them.
c   One of the best things about holidays is that you _____ get up early in the morning if you don't want to.
d   You _____ to come with me to a football match one day – I think you'd enjoy it.
e   What do you think I _____ do? I need your advice.
f   In some countries the law says, you _____ use mobile phones while driving a car.
g   My six-year-old sister goes to school but she's lucky because she _____ do any homework yet.
h   You can visit Martin, but remember the rules – you _____ be back by ten o'clock.
i   I don't think we _____ wait any longer – he's obviously not coming.

COUNTABLE/UNCOUNTABLE

Singular countable nouns have *a/an* or *this/that* or *my/your* etc. before them.

There's a car outside my house.
It's an old Mercedes.

Plural countable nouns can stand alone, or they can have words like *some*, or *four*, or *these/those*, or *my/their*, etc.

There are monkeys in this forest and some elephants too.

Uncountable nouns have no plural; you cannot use *a / an* or *1 / 2 / 3*, or *-s*.

They can stand alone (*Gold was found in California.*)
You can use *some* (*I need some petrol.*)
You can use *a cup of / a bottle of / a piece of*, etc. (*a bar of chocolate*)

Examples of uncountable words:

oil	sugar	metal	love	happiness
poetry	pepper	snow	tea	power
grass	money	politics		

Watch out!

There are some suprising uncountable nouns:

luggage   advice   information   furniture
accommodation   news   weather

Exercise 16

Look around you, and add six of the things you can see to each column below. Read the examples first.

Countable, singular	Countable, plural	Uncountable
a lamp	2 telephones	some coffee
a grammar book	some pictures	paper

(If you can't find many examples of uncountable words, imagine you are in a kitchen, looking into the fridge.)

MANY, MUCH; SOME, ANY, NO

Many and much have similar meanings: *a large number of* / *a large amount of*.
Both words are most often used in questions and negatives.

- use many with countable nouns in the plural
  How many men were there in the car?
  I don't know many people in London

- use much with uncountable nouns
  How much money have you got?
  There isn't much time left

- use **a lot of**, **lots of**, or **plenty of** (similar meanings) in positive sentences with both countable and uncountable nouns
  *I've got **a lot of** questions to ask, so I hope there's **plenty of** time.*

'Some' means 'a certain number or amount'.
It does not tell us how many or how much.

- use **some** with both countable and uncountable words.
  *I'm bringing **some** friends home, so I'll buy **some** wine on the way.*

- use **some** most often in positive sentences.

- use **any**, **not any** and **no** ... for questions and negatives
  *There **aren't any** people (or There **are no** people) of my age here. Do you know **any** clubs I could join?*

Exercise 17

Read the sentences below carefully, and then complete each one with a suitable word or phrase. There are a number of possible correct answers. All the sentences are about food.

We need some (**1**) ___meat___ and some
(**2**) _____ for tomorrow's dinner.
I don't think we've got any (**3**) _____
left; could you call in at the bakery and get some?
There isn't much (**4**) _____ in the
fridge. I'd like some for breakfast tomorrow.
How many (**5**) _____ and
(**6**) _____ are there in the fruit bowl?
Is there any (**7**) _____ left in the
fridge? Will you get some more, if not?
How much (**8**) _____ will you need for
the sandwiches?
We need a (**9**) _____ , some
(**10**) _____ , and lots of
(**11**) _____ for the weekend.

QUESTION FORMS

With the verb *to be*, the verb comes before the subject:
Where are you from?
Who was your first boyfriend?
What are you doing?
(verb ← → subject)

With other verbs

Where do you live? (auxiliary verb ← → subject)
How many hours' sleep does the average person need?
What time did you finish work yesterday?

With tenses which use *have / has / had / will,* and with words like *can / must.*
Have you ever visited Germany?
What must we do next?

Watch out!

> **Hidden ('embedded') questions**
> *Can you tell me where the station is?* (Not *Can you tell me where is the station.*)
> *I don't know how old he is.* (Not *I don't know how old is he.*)

Exercise 18

Nine of the ten questions below have a mistake in them. Decide what is wrong, and rewrite the sentences.

a How you are feeling today?
b You did enjoy your visit to the theatre yesterday?
c What you going to do when you leave university?
d How many you have got brothers or sisters?
e Have you had enough to eat?
f Can you tell me how much does this cost?
g Do you know who am I?
h Which does the best restaurant in town be?
i Are you be going to see Juventus play this weekend?
j How many languages do you can speak?

REPORTED SPEECH

When somebody reports what another person says, they don't use exactly the same words. Imagine that you and a friend are at a big, noisy railway station.

e.g. Announcer: *Platform 9 for the 18.05 to Cambridge.*
You: *What did he say?*
Your friend: *He said our train was at Platform 9. Come on!*

Direct speech means the words that people actually say.
Indirect or Reported speech means the words used to report or summarise what was said.

Look at the differences between these pairs of sentences. Look particularly for changes in verb tenses and word order.

Direct
"I'm feeling tired," said Howard
"I need a rest."
"I think I've caught a cold."
"Can I take a week off work?"
I said: "Why don't you see a doctor."

Indirect
Howard said that he was feeling tired.
He told us that he needed a rest.
He thought he had caught a cold.
He asked if he could take a week off work.
I told him to go and see a doctor.

Exercise 19

Here are some sentences about a hotel. For sentences a–d, complete the second sentence with the words that the people probably said (use no more than three words).

a The receptionist asked us what time we had left home.
She said: "What time _____ _____ home?"
b We told her that we had left at six o'clock.
We said: "_____ _____ at six o'clock".
c She asked us if we were hungry.
"_____ _____ hungry?" she asked.
d She told us that the swimming pool was still open.
"The swimming pool _____ _____ open," she said.

For sentences e and f, complete the second sentence in reported speech.

e "Please leave your passports with me," said the receptionist.
The receptionist told _____ _____ our passports with her.
f "Your rooms are on the tenth floor," she said.
She told us that _____ _____ on the tenth floor.

WORD ORDER

The usual order of words in a sentence in English is

Subject   +   Verb   +   Object

The woman   bought   a book

Verb and object are almost always together (not *She bought yesterday a book.*)

Where and *when* something happened is usually at the end of the sentence.

The woman   bought   a book   in town yesterday.

There are special rules for these words:

always	usually	often	sometimes
rarely	never	ever	just still
already	also	only	

- They come **after** the verb to be
  She isn't often late.
  We were already there.

- **After** the first auxiliary verb
  She had never seen him before.
  He hasn't always liked music.

- **Before** a single main verb
  Do you usually get up early?
  They already knew the answer.

Exercise 20

Put the words into the correct order to make sentences about travelling abroad. The first word of each sentence is in the correct position. When you've finished, the last letter of each sentence a–l will make the names of two more countries.

a   Have Everest Mount ever seen you?

b   I'm Peru trip a back to from just

c   When I a country arrive I in hire always a car

d   I'm week Iceland going next to

e   Travelling if is difficult don't the local you language speak sometimes

f   I in only Italy could day stay for one

g   I with stay in Quebec often friends

h   I'm hoping the of Leaning to see still Tower Pisa

i   I've visited never Bhutan

j   Last China two spent I summer in weeks

k   I first travel I abroad when fly class usually

l   I'm my trip already next Bolivia planning to

Appendix 1

Paper 1 Writing Test marking criteria

There are three parts in the Writing Test. Part 1 is a sentence transformation task.

In Part 2, you must write a short message of 35–45 words which must include three specific points.

You have a choice for Part 3: either an informal letter or a story of about 100 words.

Remember in Parts 2 and 3

- Keep to the word limits as much as possible: if you write a lot more (e.g. 100 words for Part 2), your 'message' will not be communicated clearly and you may lose a mark.
- Your writing does not have to be free of mistakes to get the top marks.

Marking criteria for Part 2 (35–45 word message)
5 All three pieces of information covered appropriately. The message is communicated to the reader clearly.
4 All three pieces of information covered adequately. Generally, the message is communicated to the reader.
3 All three pieces of information attempted. The reader needs some effort to understand the message. OR One piece of information not included but the other two are clearly communicated.
2 Two pieces of information not included, or not covered well enough. OR Answer may be short (20–25 words).
1 Not much that answers the question. Needs a lot of effort to understand it or may be very short (less than 20 words).
0 Totally irrelevant or incomprehensible or too short (under ten words).

Sample 1: (see Exam practice page 45 for task)

> Dear Sarah
> I received your card, thank you very much for your invitation.
> Congratulation for your engagement. I am so happy for you and David.
> I accept your invitation.
> I hope see you for the lunch next week, what do you think about Thursday about 12 o'clock in my house? Call me.
> Kiss
> Marcela

5 marks: All three pieces of information are included; the message is clear; minor mistakes are not important.

Sample 2:

> Dear Sarah
> I am wraiting this note to give my sancerely congratuleitions for your engagment party. It's a pleashure for me to asist to your party.
> I think so too is a good idea to go to eat the next week for talk about your engagment.
> Love Beno
> PS I wait your answer a.s.a.p.

3 marks: All three pieces of information attempted but the message is not always clear. The reader needs to make a bit of an effort to understand.

Marking criteria for Part 3 (100-word informal letter or a story)

The examiner will consider the following:

Does it answer the question?

How much effort does it take the examiner to read it?

How confident is the student in his/her use of language?

Is there a range of structure and vocabulary?

Is it organised, and does it use some 'linking' structures?

Do the kind and/or number of errors cause communication problems?

A mark on the scale of 0–5 is given depending on how well the student's work answers the above six questions.

Sample 1: (see exercise 4 page 49 for task)

Dear Gil

I received your letter, I hope you'll feel better. What was "Ice Storm" like?

Look, for respond at your question, I love going to the cinema with my friends.

I can spend my time n the cinema but the problem is if you don't like the film you can't turn over and choose an other film.

I like to watch moveis in the tv because I can stop the video when I want, I can change the film if I don't like the movies.

Moreover I can stay in pyjama I don't need to put on my clothes.

That's all, I hope to see you soon.

Love Monika

5 marks: Answers the question well and is always understandable. Confident use of language, good structures and vocabulary. Errors are minor.

Sample 2:

Dear Gill

Thank you for your letter.

I also have got a cold yesterday, I think we stayed at home and watched DVD is better.

But it put Chicago on the screen now. I want to watch it! I prefer it.

How about you? Shall we go to the cinema?

However if your condition is not good, we stay at home.

Up to you. Please write your response a.s.a.p.

Love Keiko

2 marks: Doesn't fully answer the question – student does not make clear whether she prefers watching films at home or cinema. Some confusion with verb tenses which make the message difficult to understand. Some evidence of linking structures. Rather short (70 words).

Sample 3: (see exercise 6 page 53 for task)

Two years ago, I decided to take karate lessons. In the course, I studied hard, so in the final that graduated with honors, and teacher acquired the certificate of merit to me, I was very happy that time. But in that coming about six months, I had not used my karate knowledge, I started thinking "Why did I study karate, it's useless, I was crazy." Until one day, when I walked on the street, suddenly, I heard someone shouted 'help'. I attempted to find it, about two minutes later, I found it in a corner of the street, I was surprised, there was a man wants to attack a woman. I was going up immediately fight with him, I used karate to attack, and I took him to the police station, so the woman told the police that I was a hero.

3·5 marks: Clear evidence of linking ideas together; but organisation would have been helped with paragraphs, and better punctuation. Message is understandable although second sentence is confused. Most past tenses used correctly. Candidate has attempted to use interesting vocabulary but not always successfully.

Sample 4:

Two years ago, I decided to lesson karate.

I visited to Dojo (where to lesson karate) near my house and join there.

At first time I was afraid of kicking someone, as time goes on, getting exciting.

One day, on the way to Dojo, I help a woman her husband hit her.

I am telling to stop them, but he didn't stop, so I throw him from my back.

Then a police phoned had arrived there.

The woman told the police that I'm a hero.

2 marks: Answers the question, but quite a number of mistakes which sometimes makes communication of the message a problem . Control of past tenses is lacking.

There is evidence of organisation and some linking structures. A little short.

Paper 3 Speaking Test marking criteria

There will be two examiners and two candidates for the Speaking Test.

Remember

- The examiners want you to do well.
- You need to say enough so that the examiners have enough language to mark.
- You are allowed to make mistakes.
- Most candidates are nervous.
- If you don't understand an instruction, ask the examiner to say it again.

The Speaking Test examiners will be marking the following:

Grammar and vocabulary

- Can you use the present, past and future tenses?
- Can you form questions?
- Do you have enough vocabulary to say what you want? If not, can you express what you want to say using other words?

Fluency and the ability to express ideas

- Can you express your ideas well enough so people can understand you?
- Are you able to answer questions with more than just a word or simple phrase?
- Can you suggest, agree, disagree, give an opinion, ask for an opinion, explain and give reasons?
- Can you keep talking (about a photograph, for example) for about a minute?

Pronunciation

- Are most of the individual sounds you make clear enough?
- Does your speaking show some appropriate linking of words, word stress, and sentence 'rhythm'?

The way you communicate with your partner (and with the examiner)

- When two of you are working together, can you show that you're able to get your partner involved in the discussion and also that you can respond to your partner's ideas?
- Do you know when/how to be a listener? It's good to listen as well as speak.
- Are you able to move a discussion forward so you and your partner come to some kind of conclusion?

	Below level	**Pass**	**Good pass**
Grammar and Vocabulary	Grammar incorrect, not enough vocabulary, so 'message' is not understandable.	Message is understood. Often small grammar and vocabulary mistakes.	Message very clear. Always understood. Some small grammar and vocabulary mistakes.
Fluency and ability to express ideas	Only able to keep connected speech going sometimes. Ideas difficult to follow, so message not understood.	Reasonably fluent using simple language. The ideas are mostly presented logically and with appropriate language.	No breakdowns in communication. Ideas are developed well and organised in a logical way.
Pronunciation	Because of poor pronunciation, the message is not understood.	Sometimes the listener has difficulty, but usually the message is understood.	The speaker is understood easily with only an occasional problem for the listener.
Communication with partner and examiner	Not enough language or understanding to develop communication with partner. May be long pauses.	Communication keeps going (maybe better at answering than asking). Some hesitation.	Able to ask and answer, so takes turns well. Has enough 'strategies' to develop the tasks.

Appendix 2

PREPOSITION + WORD

at first
at home / school / work
at last
at least
at night
at the beginning (of the film)
at the end (of the book)
at the moment

by bus / train / car / bike / plane
by cheque/credit card
by heart
by mistake
by myself

for ages / a long time
for my birthday
for the first / last time
for a visit / holiday

in a good / bad mood
in a hurry
in advance
in bed
in fact
in front of
in love
in my opinion
in public / private
in spring / summer, etc.

in the morning etc.
in the city / countryside
in the past
in my teens / 20s / 50s

on business / holiday
on a diet
on foot
on purpose
on TV / the radio / the internet
on the left / right
on the phone
on time
on top of
on your own

WORD + PREPOSITION

Verbs

agree with s'one
apologise for s'thg
apply for (a job)
argue with s'one about s'thg
arrive at college / in Paris
ask for s'thg

believe in
belong to
borrow s'thg from s'one
break down

call for s'one
check in
choose between
come in
compare with

depend on

fill in (a form)
find out s'thg

get in (the car)
get off (the train, etc.)
get on (the train, etc)
get out of (the car)
get on with s'one
get up (at 7.30)
give s'thg back to s'one
give up s'thg

hold on

invite s'one to s'thg

lend s'thg to s'one
lie down
listen to
look after
look at
look for
look forward to
look up

pay for
pick s'one up
put on (your shoes)

ring s'one back
ring s'one up

share s'thg with s'one
sit down
spend money on s'thg
stand up
stay in

take care of
take off (your coat)
talk to s'one about s'thg
thank s'one for
think about
throw away
try on (clothes)
turn / switch off
turn / switch on

wait for
wake up
wash up (the plates)
win (a prize) for s'thg
write down

Adjectives (be ...)

afraid / frightened of
different from
excited about
famous for

fed up with
good / bad at
interested in
keen on
late for
made of / in

married to
responsible for
sorry about s'thg
tired of
worried about

117

Practice Test

READING

Part 1

Questions 1–5

Look at the text in each question.
What does it say?
Circle the correct letter **A**, **B** or **C**.

Example:

0

> **To:** Toshi
> **From:** Olga
>
> Remember my biology book? I need it urgently, exam's on Friday!
> Leave it in main office – tomorrow at the latest. Thanks.

What does Olga want?

A to take her biology exam

B to get her book back

C to meet Toshi tomorrow

Answer: **B**

1

> **This footpath closed for repairs. Pedestrians please use path on opposite side of road.**

A Pedestrians should walk on the road.

B Pedestrians have to cross the road here.

C Pedestrians can choose which path to use.

2

> **Central Swimming Pool**
>
> Because of problems with the showers, the pool is closed until further notice.

There is something wrong with

A the showers.

B the pool.

C the showers and the pool.

3

To:	Gina
From:	Zoc

Like to go and see "Chicago" tonight?
If I don't hear from you, I'll see you
outside ABC at 7.30 pm. OK?

What does Gina have to do when she reads the email?

A reply immediately

B ring the cinema

C nothing

4

Had a bad start to the
holiday - our luggage didn't
turn up for 2 days! But
now - brilliant place!
Spending most of the time
water-skiing. We're thinking
of not coming home!

Why don't they want to come home?

A Because they lost their luggage.

B Because they like the place so much.

C Because they missed two days of their holiday.

5

Winter opening times

Museum open daily,
except Monday
10.00. − 18.00

You can visit the museum

A at any time.

B on any weekday.

C at the weekend.

Part 2

Questions 6–10

The people below all want to choose a TV programme to watch.
On the opposite page there are descriptions of eight programmes.
Decide which programme would be the most suitable for the following people.
For questions **6–10**, mark the correct letter (**A–H**) below.

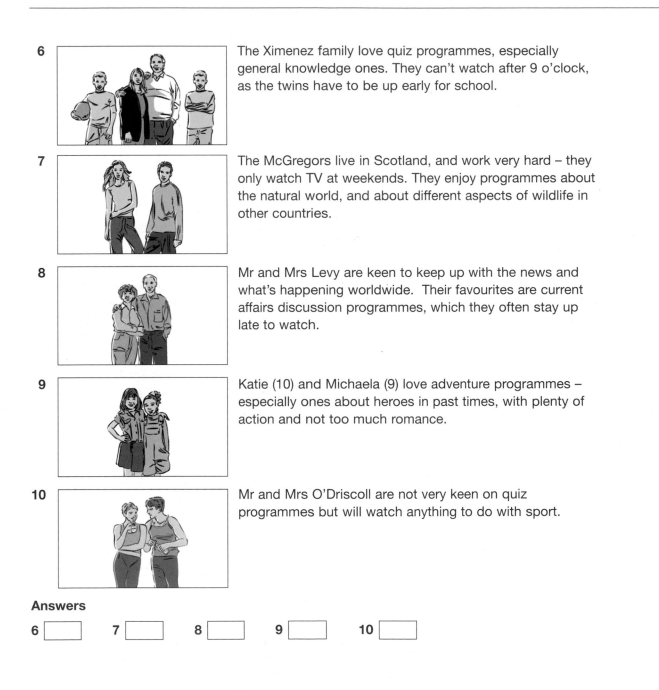

6 The Ximenez family love quiz programmes, especially general knowledge ones. They can't watch after 9 o'clock, as the twins have to be up early for school.

7 The McGregors live in Scotland, and work very hard – they only watch TV at weekends. They enjoy programmes about the natural world, and about different aspects of wildlife in other countries.

8 Mr and Mrs Levy are keen to keep up with the news and what's happening worldwide. Their favourites are current affairs discussion programmes, which they often stay up late to watch.

9 Katie (10) and Michaela (9) love adventure programmes – especially ones about heroes in past times, with plenty of action and not too much romance.

10 Mr and Mrs O'Driscoll are not very keen on quiz programmes but will watch anything to do with sport.

Answers

6 [ ]   7 [ ]   8 [ ]   9 [ ]   10 [ ]

Recommended TV programmes

A *Any Sporting Ideas?*

Not the quiz programme you expect from the name, perhaps. This late-night question-and-answer series takes viewers' suggestions for improving different sports, and experiments to see whether they would work or not. Watch out for plenty of ideas for deciding if the football crossed the line or not!

B The Very, Very Wild Show

The quality of wildlife photography is so high these days that it's easy to forget how dangerous it can be. One cameraman was almost killed while filming the episode to be shown this Sunday, in which we find ourselves face to face with an Indian tiger which seems to be about one metre away.

C Big Sister Can See You!

The latest 'reality' show begins a six-week run on Saturday, hoping to continue the success story of this new form of real-life soap opera. This time the contestants are all women, and they're not locked up in a house or left on a tropical island. Their adventures begin when ... but why don't you see for yourselves? Recommended.

D We Ask the Questions

The studio audience is carefully selected, and they certainly make the 'experts' work hard in response to their questions. There's a wide range of subjects under discussion, from heroes of sport to the news of the day! It's just a shame it's on so late at night.

E *Who Let the Dogs In?*

The latest programme in the mid-week series about Europe's changing landscape looks at the continent's newest wild animal – the dog! It sounds harmless enough, but these animals are very different from those you take for a walk in the local park. Fascinating, but not for viewers with weak stomachs.

F Ask Me Another

Many people were surprised when this programme replaced the very popular early-evening film quiz, but viewers seem to like the wider range of subjects and the unusual format, especially the part where contestants are given the answer and have to guess the question.

G MARATHON

No, not another sports programme, but the story of the Greek soldier who ran 42 kilometres after a battle in 490 BC, to deliver an important message. It's colourful and beautiful to look at, with fantastic views of the landscape, but above all the action never stops, and it's very, very exciting.

H Pop Goes Politics

How do politicians of the past compare with those of today? In this clever, but not too serious programme, we see rare pieces of film showing famous names from the last century, often doing things they probably regretted afterwards. We don't learn very much that's new, but it's very funny.

Part 3

Questions 11–20

Look at the sentences below about a holiday in Patagonia.
Read the text on the opposite page to decide if each sentence is correct or incorrect.
If it is correct, circle **A**.
If it is not correct, circle **B**.

---

11 Not many people go to Patagonia.   **A**   **B**

12 The tours are not suitable for everyone.   **A**   **B**

13 You will experience big differences in temperature during the tour.   **A**   **B**

14 The strong sun means you can wear summer clothes in Patagonia.   **A**   **B**

15 Our October tour is longer than our other ones.   **A**   **B**

16 You will see whales on the tour of Peninsula Valdes.   **A**   **B**

17 The main attraction of Ushuaia is its location.   **A**   **B**

18 Lake Argentino is famous for its beautiful colours.   **A**   **B**

19 The best way to explore the park in Chile is on horseback.   **A**   **B**

20 The cost of the tour depends on when you go.   **A**   **B**

17-day holiday in Patagonia

Patagonia, in the southernmost part of the Americas, is a wild and not much visited land, famous for its wonderful nature and great scenic beauty.

Our tour will provide a range of experiences for you but we would not recommend it to anyone who does not have a keen interest in wildlife and fantastic scenery. In many of the places we go, there is little in the way of shopping or cultural activities.

We start our tour in Buenos Aires where the climate may be warm, so pack some summer clothes. But remember when we get to Patagonia and the south it will be near freezing. You should have warm underwear with you. If you feel the cold, a waterproof anorak and a warm jacket are advisable. Lightweight walking boots are also a good choice. But ... beware of the strong sun – take suncream with you.

During our October tour, two extra days will be added (making a 19-day holiday) in order to visit Peninsula Valdes. At this time of year there is a huge variety of wildlife to be seen there – seabirds, penguins and sea-elephants. Special viewing platforms have been made from which you can stand and watch these curious animals. And if we're lucky, whales, the most magnificent sea animals of all, may be seen just off the coast.

We go on to Ushuaia, the southernmost town in the world, and part of the Land of Fire (Tierra del Fuego). Stand on the coast and look out across the ocean – apart from a few small islands, there is nothing between you and the bottom of the world!

Our next stop is Calafate, in the foothills of the Andes. From there we visit Lake Argentino, a huge lake, considered one of the most beautiful lakes in the world. The Perito Moreno Glacier, which we also visit, is a river of ice that changes colours under the rays of the sun. Watch as large bits of the ice fall from a height of 100m into the waters of the lake.

The next part of our journey takes us from Argentina into Chile where we will spend some time in Torres del Paine National Park. The park is home to guanacos, the flightless rhea bird, flamingos and the bird that symbolises the Andean region more than any other – the condor. But you can do more than just watch – why not go horse riding or trekking in the park?

The cost of the 17-day tour is £3,650 which includes all transport, accommodation and meals. For the 19-day tour in October, add a further £200.

Part 4

Questions 21–25

Read the text and questions below.
For each question, circle the correct letter – **A**, **B**, **C** or **D**.

Julie MacAndrew

I've always been fascinated by history, so being an archaeologist I'm able to dig into the past and explore all the things I'm interested in, and get paid for it. I also love the fresh air which is great because even though there is some office work, most of the time I'm outside.

My interest started when I was about eight. There was something on TV about a farmer finding some gold coins in his field, and I thought that was magic. When I was at school I was hopeless at things like languages but good at subjects like science and history. I'm lucky because at that time some parts of an ancient Roman bathhouse were discovered near my town, and during my school holidays I went along to watch and help. So when I left school, university didn't attract me – I wanted to work immediately. The man in charge offered me a job – for not much money, but I learnt a lot from him. Not just practical things but also how to get the best out of the people you're working with. That's been a great help to me.

Now, I specialise in what's called Rescue Archaeology – if a company is going to build on some land, we get there first and make a record of what's in the ground before it disappears. I have the same group of people working with me on every job – we get on very well together and have some good laughs. We're friends outside work too – some of us are members of a women's football team. But often, if I've been outside in the cold and wet all day, all I want to do is stay at home and plan my next day. When I go to bed I sleep very well!

21 What can a reader learn about Julie from the text?

   A She is equally happy working outside or inside.

   B She is surprised at how much she gets paid in her work.

   C She seems to be very happy in her job.

   D She likes exploring different countries.

22 How does Julie say that her love of archaeology began?

   A A discovery was made in a field near her home.

   B A teacher helped her to become interested in history.

   C She had always had a special interest in it.

   D She saw part of a television programme.

23 Why does Julie describe herself as 'lucky'?

   A because she was good at certain subjects at school

   B because she could earn some money during the school holidays

   C because she discovered an important Roman monument

   D because she had a chance to see archaeologists at work

24 What makes her work even more enjoyable?

   A the people she works with

   B the different places she is sent to

   C the chance to work at home sometimes

   D the opportunity to play some sport

25 If Julie wrote a book about her work, what would be the best title?

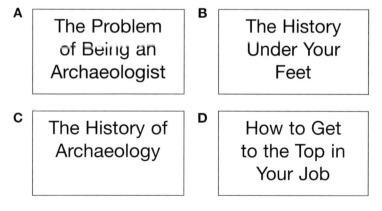

A The Problem of Being an Archaeologist

B The History Under Your Feet

C The History of Archaeology

D How to Get to the Top in Your Job

Part 5

Questions 26–35

Read the text below and choose the correct word for each space.
For each question, circle the correct letter – **A**, **B**, **C** or **D**.

Example:

0 A these   **(B)** there   **C** they   **D** those

Answer: **B**

FREE AIR TRAVEL

Most people know that **(0)** .... are many kinds of birds **(26)** .... fly long
distances every spring and autumn. This activity is known **(27)** .... 'migration'.
Scientists know **(28)** .... about where the birds fly to, and why they do it,
(29) .... there are still different **(30)** .... about exactly how the birds
(31) .... to find their way back to the same places every year.

Birds travel between the areas where they can depend **(32)** .... the best food
supply in winter, and the places where their young are born. The number of birds making
these journeys every year is **(33)** .... big that their routes are called 'flyways', and
the distances travelled **(34)** .... be amazing: there is one bird, only 350mm
(35) .... length, which in its lifetime probably travels almost a million kilometres.

26	**A** where	**B** what	**C** which	**D** who
27	**A** to	**B** with	**C** as	**D** like
28	**A** plenty	**B** some	**C** lot	**D** many
29	**A** because	**B** although	**C** so	**D** since
30	**A** meanings	**B** opinions	**C** decisions	**D** minds
31	**A** succeed	**B** can	**C** agree	**D** manage
32	**A** for	**B** of	**C** on	**D** from
33	**A** such	**B** so	**C** very	**D** more
34	**A** should	**B** can	**C** ought	**D** could
35	**A** by	**B** at	**C** over	**D** in

WRITING

Part 1

Questions 1–5

Here are some sentences about shopping.
For each question, complete the second sentence so that it means the same as the first.
Use no more than three words.
Write only the missing words.

Example:

0 Most people still prefer personal shopping to shopping on the Internet.

    For most people, shopping on the Internet is not *as popular as* **personal shopping.**

---

1 There are over 100 different shops in the new shopping mall.

    The new shopping mall .... **than 100 different shops.**

2 A few hours' shopping is tiring for most people.

    Most people .... **after a few hours' shopping.**

3 If you want a refund, you have to show your receipt.

    You cannot get a refund .... **you show your receipt.**

4 It's ages since I bought a new pair of jeans.

    I .... **a new pair of jeans for ages.**

5 Isabelle isn't going to buy the jacket because it costs too much.

    Isabelle thinks the jacket is .... **for her to buy.**

Part 2

Question 6

You have some tickets for a concert at the weekend. You want to tell the students at your college about it.
Write a notice to put on your college notice board. In your notice you should

- tell people what kind of concert it is
- give details of place, time and cost
- tell them how to contact you

Write **35–45 words**.

Part 3

Write an answer to **one** of the questions (**7** or **8**) in this part.
Write your answer in about **100 words**.

Question 7

- This is part of a letter you receive from an English penfriend.
- Now write a letter, answering your penfriend's questions.
- Write your **letter**.

> *I've been thinking about all sorts of jobs I'd like to do (and some I wouldn't like to do!). What about you? Do you have ideas about your future job?*

Question 8

- Your English teacher has asked you to write a story.
- Your story must begin with this sentence:

    Antonio picked up his guitar and began to play.

- Write your **story**.

LISTENING

Part 1

Questions 1–7

There are seven questions in this part.

For each question there are three pictures and a short recording.

Choose the correct picture and put a tick (✓) in the box below it.

Example: What time does the bank close on Fridays?

0

 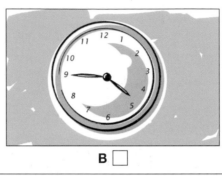 

A ✓   B ☐   C ☐

---

1 What does the woman want to buy?

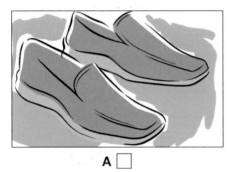 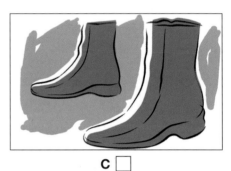 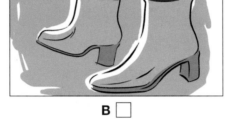

A ☐   B ☐   C ☐

2 What animals did the man see?

 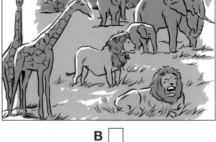 

A ☐   B ☐   C ☐

3 Which picture shows what happened?

A   B ☐   C ☐

4 How many computers does the family have?

A ☐

B ☐

C ☐

5 Where are they going for their holidays?

A ☐

B ☐

C ☐

6 Who did the woman meet?

A ☐

B ☐

C ☐

7 Which is Jane's hotel?

A ☐

B ☐

C ☐

Part 2

Questions 8–13

You will hear someone reviewing some different websites.
For each question, put a tick (✓) in the correct box.

---

8 The movieworld.com site   **A** has expensive things to buy. ☐

      B has information about the stars. ☐

      C is full of news about old films. ☐

9 What does the reviewer say about gameplay.com?   **A** There's a good variety of games. ☐

      B You have to register to play the games. ☐

      C It is a good site for beginners. ☐

10 The Deltabook site   **A** is the biggest one. ☐

      B sells more than just books. ☐

      C is cheaper than the others. ☐

11 Sportextreme.com   **A** has a very active chat room. ☐

      B covers all major sports. ☐

      C is very well designed. ☐

12 On mimusic.com you can   **A** buy tickets for concerts. ☐

      B watch live concerts. ☐

      C read the words to the songs. ☐

13 funny.com   **A** now has a different name. ☐

      B is not as good as it was. ☐

      C will soon be updated. ☐

Part 3

Questions 14–19

You will hear a man talking on the radio about Maria Silvers.
For each question, fill in the missing information in the numbered space.

> ### *Maria Silvers: businesswoman of the year*
>
> Maria was born in **(14)** .... but left when she was 11 years old.
>
> The subject she preferred at university was **(15)** ....
>
> Her first job was as a **(16)** ....
>
> In 1995, Maria and her **(17)** .... opened their first coffee bar.
>
> The number of coffee bars that she has opened so far is **(18)** ....
>
> Her business is now worth **(19)** ....

Part 4

Questions 20–25

Look at the six sentences for this part.
You will hear a conversation between a boy, Malachi, and a girl, Jasmine, about computer games.
Decide if each sentence is correct or incorrect.
If it is correct, put a tick (✓) in the box under **A** for **YES**. If it is not correct, put a tick (✓) in the box under **B** for **NO**.

		A YES	B NO
20	Jasmine understands why her father dislikes computer games.	☐	☐
21	Malachi's parents have a better opinion of computer games than Jasmine's father has.	☐	☐
22	Malachi and Jasmine both believe that playing computer games is bad for your eyes.	☐	☐
23	Malachi suggests a way for Jasmine to change her father's opinion.	☐	☐
24	Jasmine thinks that computer games should be used for management training courses.	☐	☐
25	Jasmine had a computer game which taught her to read.	☐	☐

SPEAKING TEST

Part 1 (2–3 minutes)

The test begins with a general conversation. The examiner asks each candidate questions about personal details, daily life, likes and dislikes, etc. At some time during this part, the candidates are asked to spell a word.

🎧 Listen to the examiner's questions.

Part 2 (2–3 minutes)

🎧 Listen to the examiner describing a situation.

Part 3 (3 minutes)

🎧 Listen to the examiner.

A

B

Part 4 (3 minutes)

🎧 Listen to the examiner.

Tapescript

READING

Unit 6

1

Every morning, sun or rain
Off I go to catch the train.

Need a ticket? Join the queue
Through the gate to Platform Two.

Train is crowded, dirty, late
That's a thing I really hate!

Rustling papers, coughing, yawning,
Just another Monday morning.

Walk to office, "Morning Jean"
Eighty emails show on screen.

Memos, meetings, fax and phone
Never time to call your own.

Run to catch the eighteen-ten
Sure enough, it's late again!

Turn the corner, home is near,
"Good day at the office, dear?"

WRITING

Unit 7

1

a I don't do it as much as I used to.
b People say he's getting better at it but I'm not so sure.
c It was much less expensive than I thought.
d She seems more friendly nowadays.
e It used to be the best place to go on a Saturday night.
f It's a lot smaller than the last one we had.
g It wasn't as easy as people said.
h It's the most amazing thing I've ever done.
i We've had more problems with it than we expected.

3

Dear Roger

Well, I've started my new fitness programme.
I needed to do something because I've been really lazy during the winter – too much sitting at home in front of the TV.

I've started learning to dance salsa. The classes are much more interesting than going to a gym. But it's not easy to do and I need to be fitter. For two weeks I've walked to work every day instead of getting the bus. And every time I want some chocolate I make myself drink water. The next thing will be to stop smoking but I know that's going to be hard.

I hope you'll be able to see the difference when we next meet!
Love Sabine

Unit 9

1

I was eight and it was my first experience of anything like that. My parents got George before I was born, and as I didn't have any brothers or sisters – I know it sounds silly but he was … like, a bit special. Anyway, as time passed he got slower and slower but in his head he still thought he was young. Climbing trees was still his big thing. Anyway, one day I was playing in the garden when I heard a noise in the tree above me. There was George doing his usual and then the next moment he was falling. He hit the ground and didn't move. I shouted for my Mum. But poor old George was dead. I burst into tears and cried for weeks. We never got another one – my Mum said it took me six months to get over George.

3

The day I broke my leg
It happened two years ago when I was skiing in Austria. It was a horrible day because it was snowing and I couldn't see anything. I didn't want to ski but my friends said, "Come on. This is our last day. We must go." So I went. I hadn't skied in conditions like that before so when my friends decided to go right up to the top of the mountain, I didn't join them. After about half an hour by myself, I stopped because I was cold and wet. I was getting into the cable car to go down to the village and my wonderful warm hotel when I slipped on some ice. I fell and my skis fell on top of me. I heard a terrible noise and knew something bad had happened. My leg was broken. What a way to end a holiday!

LISTENING

Unit 1

1

a 6 hours	**b** 80	**c** 26
d 38 minutes	**e** 6 kilometres	**f** 2000
g 1489	**h** £2.81	**i** 30cms
j 79%	**k** 382,650	

2

Well the answer to a) is surprising I think – it's 80. For b) it's 6 hours – that's certainly not *my* average. 6 kilometres is the answer to c) and 30cms for d). e) –, lucky 7-year-olds I say – they get £2.81 a week. Good heavens, for f) it's 79%. All that kissing in g) uses 26 calories per minute. And worldwide 382,650 babies are born every day – that's h). If you're into maths, question i), 1489 is the year that the plus and minus symbols were invented. j) is 38 minutes – and the war was between Britain and Zanzibar, and finally k) it was the year 2000 when men who worked for the Walt Disney Corporation were allowed to have moustaches.

3

Woman: Well, we started in 1992 – just two courses in that first year but now we run about 50 courses a year. The good thing about our school is we work with small groups – maximum six in any one group so you get a lot of individual help. So as long as you can swim and are over 14, then we'd love to have you.

The next course starts on June 14th and it's quite a full programme – we start at 9.30 in the morning and go on until 3 in the afternoon. The cost for a week's course, including accommodation, is 300 euros and we ask for a deposit of 50 euros when you make a reservation.

4

Man: We're trying to arrange a meeting to discuss our prices for next year. Is the 20th any good for you?
Woman: Sorry no. I can't do that or the following day, so … what about the 22nd?
Man: It'll have to be, I guess. We need to announce the new prices before the 24th so we haven't got much choice.

5

Man: Well, you see, I have still got a car but I don't drive unless I really have to. I prefer the train, actually. It's expensive but it's quicker than the coach and doesn't get stuck in traffic jams.

6

Man: Andrea, have you got a badminton racket I could borrow?
Woman: Sorry no. I don't play anymore – too energetic for me.
Man: Really? I thought you were a fitness fanatic.
Woman: Well, I do try to keep fit still with tennis at least twice a week. I enjoy all that running about and being outside. And of course the kids keep me fit.

7

Woman: Gosh, hasn't Chloe grown? How old is she now?
Man: Ten months, and just beginning to talk.
Woman: She seems very fond of that little elephant.
Man: Yeah, funny how babies really love one thing. First it was a furry cat but she lost that.
Woman: My children all loved dolls from when they were really small.

8

Man: … and then I missed the train at Cardiff and had to wait over an hour until two for the next one. So I didn't get in until quarter past five, instead of four o'clock as I'd planned. But that was just the beginning. When I got home… (fade out)

9

Man: Now where did I put my car keys? They're not in my briefcase …
Woman: Kitchen table? – they're usually there.
Man: No, I remember now, I put them on the chair, 'cos the phone rang just as I was coming in.
Woman: Well, if that's where you put them, that's where they'll be.

Unit 2

2

a Woman: Jack … close the window in the bathroom – the wind's getting really strong.
Jack: Done. Honestly, talk about changeable – we seem to have had a whole year's weather in one day today.
Woman: I know – this morning we could hardly see across the road because of the fog.
Man: Yeah, but at lunchtime I sat in the park enjoying the sun. Then on the way home from work I got caught in the rain and sat on the bus feeling very wet and miserable.
Woman: And now we've got this. England in April – how lovely!

b Man: My father worked as a lawyer in my grandfather's firm in Liverpool but he met my mother in Scotland when they were both there on holiday. She was the daughter of a factory owner from London. Both my parents came from large families, and I have a number of cousins now living in different parts of the world. I've recently become an uncle for the first time, which makes me feel terribly old.

c Woman: When I was a kid, we had a dog called Penny that we all loved but we used to argue about whose turn it was to take her for a walk – especially in winter. I can remember saying 'she doesn't need much of a walk, she's got really short legs' but that didn't work, I had to take her. One job I did like was brushing her – she had really rich brown hair and she'd sit for hours enjoying all the attention. But like most dogs, she hated having a bath – it didn't happen that often but sometimes we'd put her in the bath with some special dog shampoo and she'd bark loudly. But when she was walking by a river, she couldn't wait to get wet – funny that.

3

Recording 1
Woman: Tomatoes, and garlic – that's OK, we've got plenty of them.
Man: What about onions?
Woman: Yeah, get a kilo of onions. And half a kilo of carrots.
Man: There are still some left.
Woman: I know but I'd like some anyway.

Recording 2
Woman: OK, so see you at seven outside the cinema.
Man: No, make it inside in case it's raining.
Woman: Good point. By the hot dog stand?
Man: It'd be better by the ticket office.

Recording 3
Man: Dave heard about the concert on the Internet and he bought his tickets last week.
Woman: Good for him! I didn't know anything about it until I saw the poster in the city centre. It was really funny because Jane and I were just saying how we'd really like to see him live – and there it was!

Recording 4
Man: How did it happen, then?
Woman: It just sort of fell out of my hands. I'd just finished all the washing up and I was drying things, and I was thinking about making a cup of coffee and I don't know – the next thing I knew there were pieces of glass on the floor.

Recording 5
Woman: Well, at the end, the sun was going down and he just stood there and watched her leave. She didn't even turn round to wave goodbye. Everyone sat there, staring at the screen, expecting her to do something but no, that was it! Nobody moved for ages after the lights came on!

4

Recording 6
Man: There were eight of us and we stayed in two different hotels – ours was in the main square and the other was by the church. I liked ours best because it was a traditional-style building. Both had a view of the mountains but ours had wonderful balconies as well where we could sit and watch the life of the village. Mary's hotel was modern and had a small garden at the back but it was rather a dark place so they all used to come to our hotel.

Recording 7
Man: Do you look like your sister?
Woman: No, not really. She's tall with incredibly curly hair. And she wears glasses.
Man: Well, you're quite tall, too.
Woman: Yeah, but I've got straight hair. And another thing, I wear skirts most of the time – she nearly always wears jeans.

Exam practice

Recordings 1–7 repeated.

Unit 3

1a

1 heat	2 hot	3 hat	4 height
5 heart	6 hut	7 hurt	8 hit

1b

The climbers stayed in a mountain hut overnight before starting their journey early the next morning.

2

a I've been walking all morning.

I've been walking all morning … and my feet are tired.

b I'm going to live there … for the next three months.

c What was she doing … when you met her?

d We saw the men outside the station … and they were talking together.

e The championship medal was won … in the last match of the season.

f It's terrible that tigers are still shot … and their fur used in the fashion industry.

g It was a horrible taste … so I didn't eat it.

h Please heat the dessert … It doesn't taste so nice if it's cold.

i What made her sink so fast? … She was heavy because she was wearing all her clothes.

j She likes peas … in fact they're her favourite vegetable.

k Is there a spare seat anywhere? … Yes, there's a chair free next to Tony.

l Could you wash the baby, please? … He's been in the garden and he's dirty.

3

I'm happy to say that The Black Horse Leisure Centre, which opened last week, is great. It's taken three years to build and was originally due to open eight months ago. But problems with one of the swimming pools meant a delay.

Annual membership of the centre is £360 and that means you can use all the facilities without paying any more. Or if you prefer, you can pay £15 a month for the use of the swimming pools. But what's good about this centre is you don't have to be a member at all – you can just pay every time you go there for whatever facility you want to use – great!

And what will you find? Well, for a start there are three swimming pools, one for serious swimmers, a teaching pool, and one for children. But the big thing that the centre is very pleased about – there are six indoor tennis courts – believe it or not, these are the first indoor ones in the whole area. Then, there's a fitness studio, a sauna and a steam room.

Opening times are from 6.30 in the morning till 10.30 at night, except for Saturdays when it closes earlier at 6.00 pm. And on Sundays it opens half an hour later at 7.00 am.

There's a bar on the ground floor and a café on the first floor, although when I went, there were a few problems in the kitchen which meant having to wait for our meals. And next to that there's even a place where you can leave your kids to have fun for two hours, if they're between 6 months and 5 years.

There's a car park but for some reason it only takes about 50 cars – simply not enough for a place of this size. So instead catch a bus or tram direct from the city centre – and for this month only it's a free service.

So come on all you couch potatoes, get down to the Black Horse Leisure Centre and get fit.

Unit 4

1

Man: Well, I've got this picture of a small café with some people sitting outside, drinking. There are three tables and they're all round. On each table there is a menu card. The right-hand table has got some flowers on it. At the middle table there's a man and a woman. She's drinking coffee – holding the cup in her left hand. She's wearing jeans and sandals and a short-sleeved shirt, and nothing on her head. The man's reading a newspaper – his cup is on the table. He's wearing shorts and a stripy T-shirt, and sunglasses. There's a backpack on the floor beside him. The waiter's coming out of the door of the café holding a tray with three bowls of ice cream.

2

Woman: Well, the five cafés I'm going to tell you about are all very different.

First, there's the Queen's Lane Café which is in the High Street, quite near the city centre. It's small and always busy – not the sort of place where you can sit for hours reading the newspaper. It's very popular with university students because they cook a huge English-style breakfast there – you know eggs, bacon, sausage, beans – the lot.

OK, then there's the Grand Café, again in the High Street. You wouldn't find bacon and eggs there, although they do serve food – typical things would be smoked salmon with champagne. Again it's quite a small place, but it looks much bigger because the walls are covered in mirrors, which makes it really special. As you can probably guess, it's not cheap in the Grand Café, but a great place to go if someone else is paying for you. It's popular with people in their 20s and 30s.

About 15 minutes' walk from the centre, there's Café Coco. It's really friendly in here. Nobody minds if you stay all day. You can sit in comfortable chairs, read the newspapers, talk about the world and eat burgers or salads – or you could simply have a coffee. It's a big, noisy place that people of all ages go to.

Then there's Edgar's Café which is actually not particularly special except it's right in the city centre. So you can imagine it's very popular with people doing their shopping just to pop in for a quick snack and a drink. One unusual thing about it is that the café's outside – what about the rain, I can hear you asking? Well, it's covered by a sort of roof and in the winter they have huge outdoor heaters.

And finally there's Freud's Café in Walton Street, about 15 minutes from the centre. People walking past Freuds would never guess it was a café – it looks like a church which it was until about 20 years ago. What's interesting about this place is not so much the food or drink, but the fact that they have live music there quite often. And because it's such a big place, it's great for groups of friends to meet there.

So there you are – five cafés to choose from.

3

a Queen's Lane Café is very popular with university students because they cook a huge English-style breakfast there.

b The Grand Café is quite a small place, but it looks much bigger because the walls are covered in mirrors, which makes it really special. As you can probably guess, it's not cheap in the Grand Café.

c It's really friendly in Café Coco. Nobody minds if you stay all day. You can sit in comfortable chairs, read the newspapers, talk about the world, and eat burgers or salads – or you could simply have a coffee.

d Then there's Edgar's Café which is actually not particularly special except it's right in the city centre. So you can imagine it's very popular with people doing their shopping just to pop in for a quick snack and a drink.

e People walking past Freud's would never guess it was a café. It looks like a church, which it was until about 20 years ago. What's interesting about this place is not so much the food or drink, but the fact that they have live music there.

Unit 5

2

Man: Well, it was about three weeks that we were away in China – we went on a tour to see some of the famous places. In some ways it was silly 'cos it's such a big country and we were rushing about so much going from one place to another but the whole experience was fantastic. Anyway, we flew to Beijing and had a couple of days there getting over the flight and seeing some fantastic temples, and the first night we were there there was some sort of celebration so we stood up on the roof of our hotel and watched all these fireworks shooting up into the night sky – almost like a personal welcome!

And then from Beijing we went by coach to Badaling, to see the Great Wall. I mean I'd seen pictures of it and everything before but honestly it's just staggering – it seems to go on for ever. The light was fantastic and the red and yellow colours of the trees made it all great. I took loads of pictures. The only thing I didn't like was the number of tourists – but I suppose we were part of that – but you could walk along the wall and escape the crowds.

Then we went back to Beijing and the following morning flew to Xian. The reason everyone goes there is to see the army of Terracotta warriors – you've probably seen pictures of them – hundreds and hundreds of carved soldiers and horses all done for an early Emperor. What I didn't realise is that every single one is different – the workmen who carved them must have been incredible artists.

Well, after that we were going to fly up to Nanking to take a trip on the Yangtse River but in the end we didn't. We took the train to Suzhou instead. That was lovely, lots of beautiful canals – a bit like Venice – and peaceful gardens. Then on the train again to Shanghai – that was a bit of a contrast to Suzhou – incredibly busy and noisy and full of western-style buildings on the banks of the river. It's an important city for shopping – we were told about one shopping street about 5km long which has over 1 million shoppers every day. A nightmare! But we did visit the old city which I found fascinating – it's just a mass of tiny streets and if we hadn't had a guide, we'd have got lost for sure.

Then we flew to Guilin in the south – I hadn't expected it to be raining – normally the sun shines and the temperature is in the mid-30s. It was a pity about the weather as the following day we went on a river boat to look at the spectacular scenery – it's quite a famous place for artists.

I've nearly finished now – our last Chinese flight was from Guilin to Canton which **was** hot and from there we caught the train to Hong Kong. We had a couple of days there for shopping or whatever people wanted to do. I just sat and watched all the activity in the harbour. Then we flew home and now … now would you like to see all my photos?

3

Woman: First up there's one of Hollywood's best known films *The Wizard of Oz*. It's a musical adaptation of a classic story and is probably the best loved fantasy film of all time. It has something for everyone – wonderful strange lands, a fabulous collection of characters, songs that everyone can sing along with but above all, it's got Judy Garland acting the central character of Dorothy. It's impossible to imagine anyone else playing the part so well.

The Lord of the Rings is another fantasy which tells a big story. It's in three parts. Based on the classic book by J R Tolkien, it is a hugely successful adaptation. It's long, perhaps too long, but the special effects are some of the best – it's difficult to take your eyes off the screen for even a second in case you miss something. And the acting is great.

Monsoon Wedding is a real feel-good film. The story takes place in modern-day India, Delhi to be precise, and it centres around the preparations for a wedding in one of Delhi's high-class families. The director brings in romance, family secrets, and even some song and dance routines. The whole film is full of colour. At the end, you feel happy to be alive – or I did anyway when I first saw it on a wet Sunday afternoon in February.

The Others, starring Nicole Kidman is set in a big house. Mum (Nicole Kidman) is very strict with her two children and the three, rather strange, servants. But their lives are turned upside down by an unseen ghost of a boy who makes things happen in a very scary way. What makes this an unusual horror movie is the action in the film which is quite slow, but when something does happen it's quite shocking, except for the last scene of the film which just made me laugh. But, not a film to see if you're staying at home on your own this weekend.

Phantom of the Rue Morgue was made in 1954 and is also based on a book, this time by American Edgar Allan Poe. It's the story of a crazy Paris scientist who hypnotises a gorilla to kill beautiful women. Sounds stupid doesn't it, but I remember reading the book when I was younger and really enjoying the story. The film doesn't live up to my memory of the book. And then there's the acting – the guy who plays the detective is totally wrong for the part, and the man in the gorilla suit isn't very good either.

Exam practice

Welcome to this week's programme. Today we're looking at the story behind the film *They Shoot Horses, Don't They* which was all about a dance marathon that took place in the USA in the 1930s – a time of great economic problems when many people lost their jobs.

Young men and women entered these dance marathon competitions, where you danced without stopping for hours and hours, until only one couple remained on the dance floor – the winners! Everyone did it because they really wanted the cash prize, but some also hoped that there might be a Hollywood film producer in the audience, who would offer them a part in his next film. And for some, the free meals and being somewhere warm for a few days was the attraction.

The rules varied, but everywhere the most important one was that the dancers must never stand still. Generally, you were allowed 15 minutes of rest for every hour of dancing, but no sleep – although at some marathons one dancer could sleep if their partner held them up, and didn't stop dancing. The kind of dance they did was unimportant, although in the early days of a competition there would be some who tried to please the audience with the quality of their waltzes or tangos. But soon the only thing that mattered was surviving on the dance floor until everyone else had dropped out.

People paid between 25 and 50 cents to come and watch the dancers – sometimes up to 5,000 people were in the audience. They brought their food and drink with them and even brought gifts for the dancers. But they also laughed at them and thought the whole thing was great fun. The tired dancers, however, found it a long and painful experience.

In 1933, dance marathons were made illegal in the USA, although some businessmen kept them going until about 1946. During one competition in New York in 1940, the police came in to stop it but the organisers simply moved all the dancers onto trucks – still dancing – and drove them to a ship which then sailed out to sea. In fact, that particular competition ended when the dancers got seasick.

Dance marathons were the subject of the film *They Shoot Horses, Don't They* made in 1969. It's only two hours long but at the end of the film the audience feels almost as tired as the dancers. It's not a happy film, but it is an excellent one and received nine Oscar nominations.

Unit 6

1

a **Man:** What's your name?
Woman: Gill Kenworthy.
Man: Could you spell that, please?
Woman: Sure, G-I-double L, and my surname is Kenworthy – K-E-N-W-O-R-T-H-Y.

b **Woman:** Where do you live?
Man: 59 Juxon Avenue – that's J-U-X-O-N, Avenue.

c What's unusual about these two words? Write them down and look at them – R-E-F-E-R and M-A-D-A-M.

d And here are some things you might write at the end of a text message: write them down and work out what they could mean. Each letter represents one word: T-T-Y-L   H-A-N-D.

2

Message 1: It's Josie. Just thought I'd tell you 'cos I know you're planning your next holiday to New Zealand, there's a programme about it on TV tonight at … um … half past nine. It's called *Out and About*, BBC2 I think.

Message 2: Hi, it's Mark. Sorry, I got it wrong when we spoke earlier. About dinner. The restaurant is closed on Mondays, so we'll have to make it Tuesday instead. Ring me.

Message 3: Carole, it's Elena. I'm having a party on the 24th. It's going to be at my house – 112 Lexington Drive. L-E-X-I-N-G-T-O-N Lexington Drive. Hope you can come.

Message 4: It's Margrit, Tuesday, ten past eight. I phoned the information hotline about the tickets – there's a big price range from £10 to £45. What shall we go for? Ring me back quickly, or leave a message – 08766 327714. Tickets are selling fast.

Message 5: Carole, it's David – do you remember, your brother David! I don't think you ever listen to your messages! So I'm coming to see you on Saturday. We need to talk about Mum and Dad's Christmas present so write down some ideas.

4

Woman: We're sorry but the offices of Dawson Holidays are closed until nine o'clock on Monday. If you wish to leave a message, please speak clearly after the tone and we'll deal with it as soon as possible.

Man: I'd like to leave a message for the Customer Complaints Manager. My name's Jason Thatcher – that's T-H-A-T-C-H-E-R, address 201 Barnsley Drive, B-A-R-N-S-L-E-Y Drive, Cambridge and my holiday reference number is RY/37590. My wife and I have just come back from our holiday in the Bahamas, arranged by your company. We were staying in the Grand Hotel although we were expecting to be in the Hotel Tropicana. We were only told about the hotel change two days before we left home.

The Grand Hotel was nice but it was not near the beach and it took us at least 30 minutes by taxi to get to the capital for our evening entertainment.

I really think your company should have given us more information before we went. We found out that August is not a good month to be there 'cos the hurricane season runs from June to November. Fortunately, we didn't have a hurricane but we did have some very strong winds and a lot of rain – 10 days out of 14 it rained. I know that you're not responsible for the weather but you *are* responsible for giving accurate information to your customers.

Please write to me at the address I gave you at the beginning of this message. I'll be interested to hear your side of this story.

Unit 7

3

David: Hi, you've reached David Watkins. Sorry I'm not here to take your call, please leave a message after the tone.

Clare: David, it's Clare. Good meeting today, I thought, and some interesting applications, could be a great group! There's just one more that came in and I thought you might like to think about it over the weekend before Monday's decision. I'll just read it to you.

OK so it's from Darius Gallagher – he's 38 and divorced. He's working as a builder at the moment, which sounds useful, doesn't it? Incidentally, in his letter that he sent with the application form, he said that he used to be a teacher so he's had some experience of managing people. He's obviously quite a sporty guy – he's put down climbing, wind-surfing, sailing and … what's this … ah yes, fishing – all the sorts of sports you tend to do as an individual rather than as a team member but … who knows? Under useful interests he's got cooking, boat-building and listening to people – sounds a bit too wonderful, doesn't he? Then under any fears, he's put being with boring people. And lastly he's given himself a 4 for fitness. So that's Darius Gallagher. See you on Monday, David. Bye.

4

Woman: Now for all of you who are keen on excitement or who enjoy frightening yourselves, there are some brilliant new rides at two of Britain's theme parks.

The first one is called Air and it's at Alton Towers Theme Park. It cost £12m to build and it's a bit different from the traditional roller coaster. For a start, you're not in a carriage – the top half of your body is in a harness but your legs hang down. The machine is taken up to its highest point and you come back down to earth, face down travelling at up to 88 kilometres an hour. If you fancy trying this, then Alton Towers is open from 9.30 am to 7.00 pm until November 3rd and the cost of a day ticket is £20 for children and £25 for adults, everything included but you have to pay for your food. This new ride is going to be very popular this year so if you don't live near Alton Towers, it might be a good idea to stay in a hotel nearby and get to the theme park early so you don't have to queue. Call 089705 200606 for hotel recommendations.

Then there's Colossus at Thorpe Park. This is more of a traditional roller-coaster – in fact it's the biggest looping roller-coaster in the world. It cost £10m to make – that's £1m per loop. During the ride, you are turned over ten times at speeds of up to 112 kilometres an hour and the whole thing lasts 50 seconds. It's so fast, you don't even have time to think how terrifying it is. The entrance fee for Thorpe Park is £18 for children and £23 for adults but by making a reservation in advance you can get a discount.

Both these rides were designed by John Wardley who used to do the special effects for the James Bond movies.

Mr Wardley's very keen to know what people think of his new rides, so if you've tried them, you can write to John Wardley, that's W-A-R-D-L-E-Y, care of us and we'll pass your comments on to him.

Exam practice

Man: Tonight we're going to be looking at the career of Mark Foster, the record-breaking swimmer. So what do we know about Mark? Well, he has 31 medals at world and European level, of which 13 are gold. And seven world records in freestyle and butterfly, all of them 50m races.

Mark had swimming lessons as a child mainly, he says, because his father couldn't swim and he didn't want the same thing for Mark. Now, of course, Mark loves his sport but he says that for him swimming is a job not a hobby. When you hear about his training schedule, you can understand why he thinks this. All week he is cither in the gym, or in the swimming pool. On Wednesdays, he adds track running to his training schedule so that leaves just Saturdays for him to do all the ordinary things of life.

Obviously he has to build up his strength with food as well. Six weeks before a competition he changes his diet – at this time, he needs to lose weight but keep the power, so he eats lots of fresh fruit and vegetables, and fish.

These foods give him the sort of energy and power he needs to be able to swim at maximum speed over 50m distance. All this care and training is put to the test on the day of competition. Mark stands at the edge of the pool with the seven other men, waits for the gun to signal the start, and then dives into the water. Somewhere between 21 and 23 seconds later, it's all over.

Unit 8

2

Speaker 1: I'm Jenny. My good friend is Sally, the girl next door to me. We've been friends for ages. We do everything together 'cos we've got similar interests.

Speaker 2: My name's Rob. No-one special at the moment. But I suppose the guys I meet every Friday are my closest mates. We go out and just enjoy ourselves – nothing heavy or serious – usually spend most of the evening laughing. That's important in a friendship for me.

Speaker 3: I'm Renate and my best friend is Fifi, my cat. I realised she was my best friend when I tried to think of someone who looks pleased to see me even if I'm in a bad mood or whatever. When I come home from work in the evening, she's there, waiting for me, welcoming me home.

Speaker 4: My name's Marcus. My best friend is the woman I've been married to for the last ten years, Amy. She knows me better than anyone else and I feel very close to her. I hope she sees me in the same way.

Speaker 5: I'm Zoe and I don't have a best friend. I have a group of friends who are very important – people who are always there when I need them. I just know they'll never let me down.

Speaker 6: My name's Jack and my best mate is my brother. That might sound strange to some people but he really is the person I can talk to. There's nothing I can't tell him. He doesn't judge me – just takes it all in and then says something really helpful.

3

Speaker 1: Jenny

It's the place I enjoy going to when I want to hide or just forget about things for a while. I've got everything I need close by – walkman, magazines, a secret supply of chocolate on the little table next to me, and bottles of water – I could survive for a week there. It's my private place – nobody's allowed to come into the room unless I let them. And when it's cold – you know just lying there with the duvet over your head – it's magic.

Speaker 2: Rob

I started collecting them when I was about ten and I've kept going fairly seriously ever since – I put them all in special books – got about ten of them altogether. I specialise now in ones with flowers on and they come on envelopes and postcards from countries all over the world. I know it's a strange hobby for a sporty kind of guy like me, in fact it was ages before I told any of my friends about it – I thought they'd laugh. But actually they were quite interested – especially when I told them how much money it's worth!

Speaker 3: Renate

When I first started, Darren had been there two years and thought he knew everything. He loved not being the new boy anymore and really made my life hell for a while – making me look stupid in front of my boss, telling untrue stories about me to colleagues and even messing about with my computer so I lost some important files. Things got a bit better when he was moved to another department and I thought I could have a fresh start but somehow it didn't work out and it wasn't long before I left.

Speaker 4: Marcus

Stupid really but if I lost it, I'm sure something awful would happen. I remember when I got it – my Dad gave it to me when I started college. Actually I thought it was a bit of an old-fashioned present because everyone uses cheap biros or things like that nowadays. This one needs ink cartridges which you have to replace. Anyway, I used it in my first exam and I just enjoyed the way it moved so smoothly across the page. Funnily enough, I got my best ever mark in that exam, so now I use it all the time.

Speaker 5: Zoe

They're an older couple – retired now and they've lived in apartment 22 all their married lives. When I moved into number 23, they were very friendly. They have my spare key so when I'm away they keep an eye on things for me, and I do their shopping when I can. We don't see each other every day but I like knowing they're there, and they say they like hearing my music through the walls.

Speaker 6: Jack

I guess I was about seven or eight and I remember Maria, my best friend at the time, asking to borrow it. I didn't want to lend it to her but my mother made me. I mean I'd never seen Maria reading anything in her life so why did she want to start now? Anyway, time passed and I forgot about it until one day I looked on the shelf and it wasn't there. Next day, I asked Maria to give it back and she said she didn't know what I was talking about – never heard of it, never had it, etc. Not surprising really she stopped being my best friend from that day and since then I've been very careful with my things.

5

Conversation 1

Man: You're looking very well! Been away?

Woman: Yes – but on business. I really enjoy these trips – I just love hearing different languages around me, and all the colours, and smells, and the food …

Man: But you still had to work, didn't you?

Woman: Of course, but I don't mind that.

Conversation 2

Woman: Did you enjoy the film?

Man: No, not really. I thought it was too long, not very funny and the acting was just bad. It looked good though, particularly the scenes under water.

Conversation 3

Young boy: What's that music, grandma?

Grandmother: Beethoven's 5th symphony.

Boy: Do you like it?

Grandmother : Well, I wouldn't play it if I didn't like it, would I? I know you think I'm boring when it comes to music but I know what I like, and I like lots of different music from Beethoven to the Beatles.

Boy: Who are the Beatles?

Conversation 4

Man: I really can't see why people spend so much just to get a designer name on their jeans – unless of course they're better made, or better quality material. And anyway, everybody knows half of them are cheap copies, not the real thing at all. I prefer to spend my money on other things.

Unit 9

2

Peter: Well, thank goodness that's over. I don't think I've done very well.

Joe: You always say that after exams, Peter. You'll be fine.

Peter: Mmm, we'll see. I bet I won't get the mark I need for college.

Joe: Well, there's nothing you can do – forget it for the moment. Think about your trip to India instead.

Peter: Yeah, that's brilliant, isn't it?

Joe: When are you off?

Peter: In ten days. I can't wait to get there.

Joe: And you're going to stay for …?

Peter: Haven't decided really – I've got an open return ticket. I could be away for five or six months but I've got a bit of a problem with Olivia. You know she doesn't want me to be away all that time. Says a month is long enough.

Joe: It's a really long way to go just for a month. I mean, who knows when you'll get another opportunity like this. I think you should stay as long as possible.

Peter: Yeah, you're right.

Joe: I'm really sorry I can't come with you but …

Peter: So am I. I'd hoped you'd be able to but I know you have to work and earn some money this summer.

Joe: Mmm, unfortunately. So just think of me in some boring office while you're riding on an elephant or lying on some fabulous beach.

Peter: OK.

Joe: And don't you worry about Olivia – I'll look after her.

Peter: What exactly do you mean?

Joe: It's all right – I'm only joking. Let's go and have a drink.

Peter: I can't now but I'll meet you tonight in The White Horse.

Joe: OK.

3

Conversation a:

Nick: So how did Carolyn react when you asked her about borrowing the money?

Andrea: She was very nice about it – said she understood why I needed it and she'd think about it.

Nick: Sounds possible then.

Conversation b:

Jamie: What do you think she'll say?

Ivana: I dunno. She'll be upset I guess.

Jamie: I wish I didn't have to tell her.

Ivana: Someone's got to.

Conversation c:

Marta: I've got to get this letter in the post by 12 o'clock or it'll be too late. Is it still raining?

Sam: 'Fraid so. But look, why don't I take it for you – the Post Office is on my way home.

Marta: Oh, would you, Sam, that'd be really kind.

4

Alex: Where would you like to go this weekend, then Martina? Out into the country, or are you happy to stay in town?

Martina: Well, I suppose we really should get out in the fresh air – the weather forecast's very good. It'd be a shame to stay inside watching the telly … although there *is* some really good sport on today and tomorrow.

Alex: How about going to the zoo? It's ages since I've been there. I quite fancy that for a change.

Martina: Yeah, why not? The only thing is, I'm not really sure how I feel about zoos. I know they help wild animals in some ways, but I hate seeing wonderful animals like tigers shut up in little cages for people to stare at.

Alex: Well, it doesn't have to be like that. I know what we'll do. We'll go out to Woburn. They don't have any cages there, the animals live in the park, and wander around just like they would in the natural world.

Martina: That's the safari park, or wildlife park or whatever it's called, isn't it? Where they have people driving around in cars painted to look like zebras, and they come and rescue you if your car breaks down. And the monkeys all jump on your car and pull bits off.

Alex: You can laugh … but they do a serious job there, too. They've got animals there that you don't see anymore in the wild. They've helped to keep them alive.

Martina: Well, it all sounds like a good idea, but there's just one thing …

Alex: What's that?

Martina: You know I said the weather was going to be good? Well, how do you feel about sitting in a car for hours with the windows closed because there are wild animals all around you, and the sun's beating down on the roof of the car, and …

Alex: OK, OK, I give in! Why don't we just stay at home for the weekend. It'll be a lot cheaper … and I can go for a walk.

Martina: And I can enjoy my sport on the telly.

Exam practice

Mary: Are you all right, Jack? You look a bit pale.

Jack: I'm OK, but some guy has just stolen my mobile phone. I was just texting a friend and he came up behind me, took it out of my hand and ran off.

Mary: No! But you know, I can't honestly say I'm surprised. The same thing happened to Carol and Ian last month.

Jack: What – just taken out of their hands?

Mary: Yeah.

Jack: This was my father's phone. What am I going to say to him? He'll be so mad with me.

Mary: He won't … I mean it wasn't your fault.

Jack: Well, it was really. I mean, the college have notices all over telling us to be careful about mobile phone thieves.

Mary: True. Did you see who it was?

Jack: Not clearly, but I think it was one of the students here – I'm sure I've seen his face around college.

Mary: Are you going to tell anyone about this – at college, I mean?

Jack: I dunno.

Mary: I think you should. If nobody reports a crime, how can they do anything to stop it?

Jack: Mmm. … I bet my Dad'll ring the college office to complain about the lack of security in the college or something.

Mary: Yeah, he's good at saying what he thinks your Dad, isn't he? Hey, I've just thought, what about the security cameras – they might have got the whole thing on film?

Jack: Oh yes, good thinking! Perhaps I'd better go and report it to the office after all.

Mary: Shall I come with you for support?

Jack: Thanks.

Mary: By the way, why were you using your Dad's phone and not your own?

Jack: Hummm, I lost mine at the weekend – left it on the bus I think.

Mary: Oh Jack!

SPEAKING

Unit 1

1

a, e, g, i, j, k, q, r, u, v, w, x, y, z

3

F-a-b-r-i-c-e; J-a-v-i-double t-e; S-a-s-k-a-t-double o-n; Q-u-e-b-e-c

5

Man: Good morning. My name's David Clarke and this is my colleague, Hannah Black. She's just going to listen to us. Could you tell me your name, please?
Woman: Bianca.
Man: What's your surname?
Woman: Visconti.
Man: How do you spell it?
Woman: V-I-S-C-O-N-T-I.
Man: Thank you. Where are you from, Bianca?
Woman: Italy, from the capital, Rome.
Man: And what do you do in Rome?
Woman: I'm a student at the university. I'm studying economics.
Man: Have you travelled to any other countries?
Woman: Yes, I've been to Spain and Poland.
Man: And where would you like to travel in the future?
Woman: I'd like to go to Portugal – that's where my best friend lives.
Man: Tell me something about your family?
Woman: Well, there's my mother and father, and I've got two brothers, Pierluigi and Marco – both of them older than me.
Man: Thank you.

Exam practice

Examiner: Student A, what's your name? And Student B, what's your name?

Student A, where are you from? Do you like living there?

Student B, where are you from? Have you always lived there?

Now A, do you work or are you a student?

How important is English for your future, do you think?

And B, what are you doing at the moment – working or studying?

Would you like to learn another language, apart from English?

Back to you A, let's think about music. What kind of music do you like listening to? What's your favourite musical instrument?

And B, thinking about keeping fit, what kind of exercise or sport do you usually do? What other things do you do to try to keep fit?

A, tell me something about what you usually do at weekends.

And B, tell me something about the kind of job you would like in the future.

Thank you.

A, you said your family name was … . Could you spell that, please?

And B, you said you came from … . Could you spell that, please?

Thank you. Now in the next part of the test … (fade)

Unit 2

4

Man: Mm, I don't think a theme park is a good idea because it's not very interesting for old people.
Woman: But their grandchildren would probably like it. I suppose they might choose the safari holiday if they're keen on animals.
Man: Yes, but a holiday on a cruise ship would be best, I think – good food, not much walking and popular with people of their age.

5

Your friend is packing his car to go on a summer camping holiday by the sea. He wants to take a lot of things, but there isn't enough room in his car. Talk together about how necessary all these things are for him and then decide which four things he doesn't need to take with him.

Unit 3

2a

a   Shall I start?
b   Who's going to start – you or me?
c   Shall we start with this one?
d   Would you like to begin?
e   I'll go first.

2b

Examiner: … right so, here's a picture with some ideas to help you.
Man: OK, so we have to talk about this man – mmm interesting.
Woman: Would you like to begin?
Man: OK, if you like. This one is quite funny. Shall we start with this one then?

3

a)   What about this one?
b)   What do you think about this one?
c)   What do you think we should choose?
d)   Why don't we choose a cheaper one?
e)   I think we should choose this one, don't you?
f)   Do you think this is a good one?

5

Examiner: I'm going to describe a situation to you. Your town has some money to spend on something new for the area. Talk together about what you think would interest the people of the town and then decide what new thing would be the most popular. Here's a picture with some ideas to help you.
A: Who's going to start – you or me?
B: I'll go first, if you like. Well, a car park. I don't know if the town needs a car park. I think the car drivers would like one because it's always difficult to find a place to park in the centre.
A: Yeah, but it's not very exciting is it? What about a statue? I suppose it might be nice, depends what it is.
B: Not so good if it's a politician or someone like that. Not everybody likes politicians.
A: That's true. A fountain might be good. I think it's good to have some water in the city.
B: I think so too. But it's just something to look at, isn't it? Do you think a place for skateboarding is a good idea? It'd probably be very popular with young people – perhaps there's not much for them to do in the town.
A: Mmm maybe, let's look at the others. A park with trees and places for people to sit. Quite good. What do you think?
B: I think it would be popular with a lot of people – probably more than the skateboard place. How about the swimming pool? Everyone can use that.

A: Well, we have to make a decision. I think the park or the swimming pool. What about you?
B: Let's go for the swimming pool, 'cos it's good to have a place where you can do some exercise and enjoy yourself as well.
A: OK, I agree.

Exam practice

You have agreed to look after a seven-year-old child for a day. Talk together about what would be interesting to do with the child and then decide which would be the most enjoyable. Here is a picture with some ideas to help you.

Unit 4

4

In this picture there's a woman. She's about 30 I think, and she's got dark hair that's quite long. She's wearing a black coat or something. And she's laughing.

In this picture I can see a boy and he's got his arms up in the air. He's probably about seven or eight years old. He's got dark, curly hair and he's wearing an orange T-shirt.

Unit 5

5

Student A: Well, I can see two people and they're listening to something. They might be in a train or a plane – probably a train 'cos I can see something out of the window.

She's got things on her head and he's trying to listen as well. Actually, they're rather big. Anyway, they look happy so they might be listening to some music that they like. They are both holding something in their hands but I don't know what those things are. She's wearing a grey sweater and jeans and he's got a blue jacket on. It doesn't look very warm – maybe it's winter time.

Student B: In this picture there are some people playing music outside. There are two men and one is playing – I don't know what it's called. Is it a trumpet or something … I dunno. One man is wearing jeans and a white T-shirt and the other man has jeans on and a blue shirt. Behind them are some big, tall … for the building. There are lots of people around and they're all listening to the music, I think.

Exam practice

Examiner: Now, I'd like each of you to talk on your own about something. I'm going to give each of you a photograph of people and food.

Student A, here's your photograph. Please show it to Student B, but I'd like you, Student A, to talk about it. Student B you just listen to Student A. I'll give you your photograph in a minute.

So Student A, please tell us what you can see in the photograph.

(pause tape for completion of task)

Now Student B, here's your photograph. It also shows people and food. Please show it to Student A and tell us what you can see in the photograph.

Unit 6

Exam practice

Your photographs showed people enjoying themselves on holiday. Now, I'd like you to talk together about the places you like for holidays and why, and where you'd like to go in the future.

PRACTICE TEST: LISTENING

There are four parts to the test. You will hear each part twice. For each part of the test there will be time for you to look through the questions and time for you to check your answers. Write your answers on the question paper. You will have six minutes at the end of the test to copy your answers on to a special answer sheet. The recording will now be stopped.
Please ask any questions now, because you must not speak during the test.
Now look at Part 1.
There are seven questions in this part. For each question there are three pictures and a short recording. Choose the correct picture and put a tick in the box below it.
Before we start, here is an example.

What time does the bank close on Fridays?

Man: We're sorry but the Northern Bank is now closed until Monday. Normal opening hours are from quarter to nine to five o'clock Monday to Friday and until one o'clock on Saturdays. Thank you for calling Northern Bank.

The first picture is correct so there is a tick in box A.
Look at the three pictures for question 1 now.
Now we are ready to start. Listen carefully. You will hear each recording twice.

One: What does the woman want to buy?

Woman: I can't wear those flat shoes I've got with these trousers, they wouldn't be right. I need to go shopping for some boots with a heel.

Man: You've got some boots.

Woman: Yeah, but they haven't got a heel.

Now listen again.

Two: What animals did the man see?

Woman: Any lions on your trip?

Man: Yes, loads and elephants. We were hoping to see rhinos but no luck this time.

Woman: Giraffes are the animals I'd really like to see.

Man: Yeah, me too.

Now listen again.

Three: Which picture shows what happened?

Man: Well, it was raining and there was this car coming towards us. It seemed to be in the middle of the road, so we moved over towards the side, and that's when we hit the lamp-post. And would you believe it, the car behind just passed us without stopping.

Now listen again.

Four: How many computers does the family have?

Man: Have you still got that old computer?

Woman: Yes, we all use it – actually we need to get a new one, it's not really powerful enough. But Lexie's got her own laptop that she can't live without – so she says. Now Marco wants a laptop as well, so I'm not sure what to do.

Now listen again.

Five: Where are they going for their holidays?

Woman: You're right, walking in the mountains last year wasn't a great success. That was my idea, wasn't it?

Man: Yeah, I wanted to go to a beach somewhere, remember?

Woman: Let's do that this year, then.

Man: Great. Sure you don't want to go on a cruise or something?

Woman: No, I don't.

Now listen again.

Six: Who did the woman meet?

Woman: He's great. We met at a party. He's quite tall with curly hair and a beard.

Man: You said you didn't like men with beards.

Woman: No, I said moustaches I didn't like.

Man: Fair hair?

Woman: No, really dark. I'm seeing him again on Saturday.

Now listen again.

Seven: Which is Jane's hotel?

Man: We've got a postcard from Jane in Hawaii – she's put a cross to show us her hotel.

Woman: Let's have a look. Mmmm, she won't be very happy, she wanted a view of the sea.

Man: Well, she's got the river instead.

Woman: At least it's got a swimming pool. That'll please her.

Now listen again.

That is the end of Part 1.

Now turn to Part 2, questions 8 to 13.

You will hear someone reviewing some different websites. For each question, put a tick in the correct box.

You now have 45 seconds to look at the questions for Part 2.

Now we are ready to start. Listen carefully. You will hear the recording twice.

Welcome to this week's Website Review. Today I'm going to tell you about six different websites.

First of all, for everyone who loves films and the cinema, there's movieworld.com. This is a brilliant site which tells you all about the latest films. There are interviews with the stars and a place for you to send your opinions about these new movies. There's also an on-site shop where you can buy everything from old film posters to the latest DVDs, which are much cheaper than in the shops.

If you enjoy playing games on your computer, then try gameplay.com. There's enough to keep you busy for hours from board games and puzzles to sports and action games. It's also got good links to other games sites which are easy to use. Some of the other sites have more modern games than gameplay.com but with quite a lot of them, you have to register before you can play.

Then there's the Deltabook site – it was the first and is probably the most well-known site where you can buy books online. Most other book sites have copied what they do but in my opinion they are still the leaders. It now has excellent sections for music, gifts and games and a children's section which is aimed at parents. For books, there are better prices on other sites.

Do you like exciting sports? Then log on to sportextreme.com where you can learn about everything from skydiving to white-water rafting. Each sport has its own section with lots of information about the sport, photos, etc. They're thinking of setting up chat rooms too in the next few weeks. The site is fantastic to look at – in fact it's worth a visit just for the design even if you're not interested in extreme sports.

Mimusic.com is a great new site if you're a rock fan. It's a fun site but the best thing in my opinion is you can get the words of lots of songs on screen, and they're sung by little cartoon characters which have been designed to look like the real singers. But don't expect to find more traditional things like concert tickets, interviews, or photos.

And finally, if you're thinking of logging on to funny.com to have a laugh at some jokes, don't bother. It really shouldn't be called funny.com because it isn't – funny that is. It used to be a great site to find stories, jokes, cartoons but I don't think it has been updated since it started – the jokes are rather old and it's a bit slow. Try laugh.com instead.

So, that's it for this week – more website news next week.

Now listen again.

That is the end of Part 2

Now turn to Part 3, questions 14–19

You will hear a man talking on the radio about Maria Silvers. For each question, fill in the missing information in the numbered space.

You now have 20 seconds to look at Part 3

Now we are ready to start. Listen carefully. You will hear the recording twice.

Man: Hello and welcome to the latest in our series on successful businesswomen. Today we're looking at the career of Maria Silvers, the founder of a chain of coffee bars. She comes from Nigeria but when she was 11 her family moved to London. Her family, particularly her father who was an oil executive, filled her with a belief in hard work. Maria studied politics and economics at university but she wasn't particularly keen on politics. After leaving university, she travelled for a couple of years and then became a teacher. When her father died, she went to New York for a break and every morning she'd get up and go to a coffee bar and drink cappuccinos. When she got back to London, she realised that there was nothing like those coffee bars so she decided to give up her job and do something about it – not an action she felt her father would have liked. Together with her brother she opened the first coffee bar in 1995 and success was quick. They called the chain 'Coffee Dream'. She says she's like her father – whatever she does she wants to be good at it and she admits that she's not the easiest person to work for. But she's proud of her success which is still growing, with plans to open 80 more bars in addition to the 85 that she already has. And still Maria is only 33 years old. The company now has a value of £18m which is remarkable when you think that Maria had only £20,000 to start the business.

Now listen again.

That is the end of Part 3.

Now turn to Part 4, questions 20–25.

Look at the six sentences for this part. You will hear a conversation between a boy, Malachi, and a girl, Jasmine, about computer games. Decide if each sentence is correct or incorrect. If it is correct, put a tick in the box under A for Yes. If it is not correct, put a tick in the box under B for No.

You now have 20 seconds to look at the questions for Part 4.

Now we are ready to start. Listen carefully. You will hear the recording twice.

M: Jasmine, *you* like computer games, don't you?

J: Yeah, love 'em, but my Dad isn't too keen on them. I dunno why, I can't see why it's a problem if I want to spend an hour or so playing them in my room, but he seems to think there's something wrong with me.

M: My Dad's not really like that, and my mum really encourages me – she even has a go herself when she thinks nobody's watching.

J: Dad keeps telling me it's bad for my eyes. I tell him that if that's true then so's using *his* computer on the train every day, adding up figures or whatever for his work.

M: And anyway, I think playing games on your computer or your mobile is better for your eyes than reading books or doing figures. I mean, with games, your eyes are always moving around, not just focusing on one thing all the time. Why don't you tell your Dad that scientists have just discovered this?

J: Brilliant – he's bound to believe it then! And another thing – all these people who talk about teenagers playing computer games all day instead of learning things – what they don't realise is that you often do learn things …

M: That's right, and games are getting better all the time. I mean, the ones that let you make decisions about what happens, I'd say they're really educational.

J: Yes, almost like the management training exercises that my Dad has to do. Actually I learnt to read because of a computer game – there was this really good one – called 'Civilisation', and it had all these little messages popping up on screen, and if you couldn't read them you couldn't play, so …

M: Wow, that should impress your dad – have you ever told him?

J: D'you know, I'm not sure I have …

That is the end of Part 4.

You now have six minutes to check and copy your answers onto the answer sheet.

PRACTICE TEST: SPEAKING

Part 1

Examiner: What's your name? How do you spell your surname? Where are you from?
What do you like about living in (name of candidate's town/country)?
What do you do when you're not working or studying?
Do you use a computer? What do you use it for?
Do you watch TV? What kind of programmes do you like?
Have you got any plans for the weekend?

Part 2

Examiner: I'm going to describe a situation to you. Your college is producing a new brochure to show what life at the college is like. Talk together about the pictures you think should be in the brochure and those which you think are not necessary.

Part 3

Examiner: Now, I'd like each of you to talk on your own about something. I'm going to give each of you a photograph of people enjoying themselves.

Student A, here is your photograph. Please show it to Student B, but I'd like you Student A to talk about it. Student B, you just listen to Student A. I'll give you your photograph in a moment.
Student A, please tell us what you can see in your photograph. [approximately 1 minute] Thank you.

Now Student B, here is your photograph. It also shows people enjoying themselves. Please show it to Student A and tell us what you can see in the photograph. [approximately 1 minute] Thank you.

Part 4

Examiner: Your photographs showed people enjoying themselves. Now I'd like you to talk together about the things you enjoy doing and the different times of the year you like doing them.

Answers

READING

Unit 1

1
Drink: f   Food: b, c   Clothes: g   Medicine: d, e

2
a Don't
b can't
c off
d don't; with *or* who have
e more; to
f mustn't
g at *or* from
h careful

3
1 It's a good idea. (B)
2 Switch off the lights. (A)
3 To buy a permit. (A)
4 They want to speak to anyone who saw the
   accident. (C)

4
Possible answers
a Do not talk to the driver when the bus is moving.
b Maximum 20 people.
c Mind the step.
d Sam: I've gone to my mother's.

Supplementary Activities

1
Possible answers
a You can get information here.   b Weight training,
7.00 pm every night.   c You can use mobile phones
here.   d People in wheelchairs are welcome here.
e Cheer yourself up with one of our pizzas.   f Food
served here.   g The shop will re-open at 2.00 pm.

2 a Store this bottle in an upright position.
    b CCTV cameras are used in this building.
    c All visitors must report to reception.
    d Passengers should keep their luggage with
       them at all times.

Unit 2

1 *Possible answers*
email   fax   phone   mobile   postcard
internet chat room   2-way radio   sign language
face-to-face conversation   body language

2
b 8   c 4   d 6   e 3   f 9
Possible answers
Notice 1: Because he/she wants to sell the guitar
          quickly.
Notice 2: Yes, because of the bills (electricity, etc.).
Notice 3: No, you can just come along on the day.
Notice 4: If you're having trouble with your home
          computer.
Notice 5: The person must have some experience of
          babysitting.
Notice 6: They are going to open for longer so they
          need more staff.
Notice 7: Because he's not at his normal address.
Notice 8: Her notes, her work and other papers.
Notice 9: Room 43 (the normal room).

3
1 A   2 C   3 B   4 B   5 B   6 C   7 A   8 C   9 C

Supplementary Activities
Student's own answers

Exam practice
1 B   2 C   3 B   4 A   5 A

Unit 3

1 *Student's own answers*

2
Text 1
a not having enough sleep   b Thomas
Text 2
c the activity   d Richard
Text 3
e very good – she sounds very confident
f Davina
Text 4
g not very much – they'll do things together
h Maddy

145

3

1 A, B　**2** B, C　**3** C, E　**4** E, F　**5** A, C, F　**6** B
7 D

4

1 F　**2** D　**3** E　**4** C

Supplementary Activities

Unit 4

1 To Josh from Marcus

2

a everyday lives　**b** the sea　**c** (sailing) adventures
d modern day true stories (answers in any order)
e science fiction　**f** believable　**g** short stories
(answers in any order)　**h** Far Eastern culture
i people writing about their own lives
(autobiography)　**j** women writers (answers in any
order)　**k** natural world　**l** country way of life
m the past (answers in any order)

3
Book A ✓ ✗　Book B ✓ ✗ ✓　Book C ✓ ✓ ✓

Supplementary Activities

a To Martina from Felipe
b To Marcus from Emma
c To Emma from Martina
d To Felipe from Josh

Exam practice

1 G　　　**2** C　　　**3** F
4 A　　　**5** D

Unit 5

1 *Student's own answers*

2

a F Mis-match: <u>for the weekend</u>　**b** T
c T　**d** F Mis-match: asking for <u>money</u>

3

a complete a sentence　**b** the Phindha Mountain

Lodge　**c** new, they're the kind of animals that lived
here before　**d** it is possible　**e** served, only where it
will be cooked　**f** safari laundry　**g** before June 30;
during certain holiday periods

Supplementary Activities

1

a F Mis-match: <u>lived</u>　**b** T
c F Mis-match <u>had an accident</u>

2

Possible answer
I love travelling and I'm really interested in wild
animals.

Unit 6

1 **a** queue　crowded, dirty, late train
too much work　always in a hurry

2
a feel guilty　**b** live longer　**c** good for
d doesn't give　**e** put on　**f** focus *or* think

3 **Student A**

a lost; running
b died
c two; agreement
d smoking

Student B

a difficult; fast
b before
c disagreed
d record

Supplementary Activities

1 T (b)　**2** F (c)　**3** F (f)　**4** T (e)　**5** T (a)　**6** T (d)

Exam Practice

1 T　**2** F　**3** F　**4** T　**5** F　**6** F　**7** F　**8** T　**9** F　**10** T

Unit 7

1 *Student's own answers*

2
a question 4　　**b** question 3
c question 6　　**d** question 5

3
a his dog　**b** sleeping　**c** the state of the world
d planning a meal　**e** He thinks it's not an important
part of his life, but he enjoys ironing.

4 **a** D　**b** A　**c** C

5 **2** f　**3** b　**4** d　**5** a　**6** c　**7** g

6 1 A   2 D   3 A   4 B   5 A; the letters spell TENTS.

Supplementary Activities

1 *Student's own answers* e.g. What happens about school? What are the best things about living in Botswana? What sort of research are the scientists doing with the lions?

2 1 A   2 C

Unit 8

1 *Student's own answers*

2 Kate's story

a had to mend clothes; plain dresses; aprons to keep clothes clean; plenty of underwear

b 2 kms from home; teachers were strict; boys and girls taught separately

c boys and girls separated; not allowed to talk to boys; knew nothing about sex until she was 15; shocked by diagrams

d she helped her mother in the house so didn't have time to go out

e D   **f** A   **g** C   **h** C

Debbie's story

a mini-skirts popular; spent all her pocket money on clothes

b all-girls school; not great; housecraft classes useless; couldn't do woodwork which she wanted to do

c no boys at her school; hard to meet boys except at the cinema

d didn't have to do much – just keep room tidy

e B   **f** C   **g** A   **h** B

3 1 D   2 B   3 A   4 A   5 C

Supplementary Activities

Student's own answers

Exam practice

1 B   2 B   3 C   4 A   5 D

Unit 9

1 **b** attic – because all the others are names for the same room

c balcony – because it's part of a house and all the others are part of the garden

d tent – because all the others are buildings

e sink – because all the others are electrical appliances (or have food in them)

f shelf – because all the others are necessary parts of a room

2 'Quantity' words

1 lot / number   2 every / each   3 several / some   4 lots / plenty   5 much / enough

3 *Student's own answers*

4 **a** remember
'to remind someone' means 'to make them remember'. Compare:
Remind me to buy John's birthday present.
I must remember to buy John's birthday present.

b tell
Compare:
David said (to me) that he was hungry.
David told me that he was hungry.

c do
'do' is very often used to talk about work or jobs, and 'make' is often used to talk about building, creating things. But there are many confusing areas!
Compare: *She did her homework quickly.*
        Then she made a cup of tea.

d leave
'let' means 'to allow something to happen'
Compare: *Ellie sat there and let everyone else do the work.*
        Ellie watched everyone leave the room.

e rob
You steal things and rob a place.
Compare: *He robbed the old man's house and stole his money.*

f trips
'travel' is most often used as a verb (or gerund) in English.
Compare: *I'd like to travel into space.*
        A trip into space will cost at least $10m.

g view
'scenery' is the natural appearance of a place and is an uncountable noun.
Compare: *The scenery in the Andes is breathtaking.*
        We had a great view of the mountains from our hotel.

5 1 flying (going)   2 between   3 must (the whole text is about how unusual a plane is as a home so it has to be a 'strong' modal)
4 bought   5 few   6 stole/took
7 every/each   8 where   9 let
10 number (hundreds etc.)
1 C   2 D   3 D   4 B   5 D   6 C   7 A   8 C   9 D   10 D

Supplementary Activities

1

a *doing* housework   **b** is *on* the second floor
c *a lot/lots* to buy   **d** to the *chimney*
e correct   **f** *All (of)* the rooms
g the glass *off* the table   **h** There's *nothing* / *something* wrong
i a chicken *in* the oven   **j** the *dishwasher* does the washing-up for you *or* the washing machine does the *washing* for you

2 *Possible answers*
turn on/off: the lights, the TV, the computer, the radio, the oven
sit on: a chair, a sofa, a bed, a cushion, the floor
open/close: a door, a window, a gate

Unit 10

1 *Possible answers*
to make, borrow, lend, spend, save, invest, waste, steal, win, lose, find, pay for, inherit, print

2 **1** on **2** for **3** at **4** from **5** At **6** from
7 on **8** on
seven money verbs: invest (in) / pay for / earn / lose / borrow (from) / make money / spend (on)

3 **1** because **2** and **3** when **4** then **5** unless
6 since **7** so **8** or

4 *Possible answers*
1 news   **2** becoming / getting / being
3 arrived   **4** looking / searching
5 grew / changed / developed   **6** earned / had / made
7 price / cost   **8** places
9 way   **10** famous / important

Supplementary Activities

1 **a** Money makes the world go round.
b The best things in life are free.
c Money doesn't buy happiness but it helps.

2 **2** by (g) **3** by (e) **4** about (b) **5** for (c)
6 about (a) **7** with (d)

Exam practice

1 D **2** A **3** B **4** A **5** C **6** B **7** D **8** A **9** C **10** D

WRITING

Unit 1

1 When was your last holiday? Where did you go? Have you got / Do you have any plans for this year? Where would you like to go if you had the chance?

2
b It's been great weather.
c It's only rained once / (for) one day.
d The city is very interesting.
e There's a wonderful/great swimming pool in the hotel.
f Hope you haven't forgotten I'll be in Oxford next week.
g Give my love to your brother.

3

everybody hates	nobody likes
not allowed	can't
If I were you	Why don't you
how much	cost
name	is called
What about	Let's

b the name of
c much does the trip cost?
d this camera belong to?
e not allowed to smoke on the coach.
f Nobody
g Let's go for

4
b since **c** have travelled **d** haven't decided
e a few **f** far from **g** built **h** visit **i** has been
j has (got) **k** chose the furniture
l near (to) / close to

Supplementary Activities

Possible answers

Student A
a go to the cinema tonight (What about going …)
b I started learning English … (I've learnt/been learning English …)
c My mobile … (… stole my mobile yesterday).

Student B
a Who does this book … (… is this book?)
b I haven't had a holiday … (… since I('ve) had a holiday).
c My house is not far from yours. (My house is quite near (to) yours.)

Unit 2

2

b wasn't allowed to colour my hair
c Not many (of the) people I know
d I haven't changed my hairstyle for
e lend my clothes to
f Everyone likes
g There isn't anyone/anybody in my class *or* There is nobody in my class
h think trainers are better than
i I only wear sunglasses

3

a as   **b** don't buy   **c** more than
d old enough   **e** too busy   **f** the best
g do you want   **h** don't get   **i** are you wearing

4

b comparison (to compare)   **c** marriage (to marry)
d argument (to argue)   **e** choice (to choose)
f arrival (to arrive)   **g** invitation (to invite)
h weight (to weigh)   **i** explanation (to explain)

5

a invitations to
b the arrival of
c couldn't (didn't) choose
d argument between
e explained

Supplementary Activities

Student's own answers

Unit 3

2

b don't need/don't have
c could choose
d must have
e ought to be
f you don't
g unless you

3

b did you meet
c as well with
d I wouldn't
e met
f gave
g more opportunities
h do you want
i don't have /don't need
j since I / since I have
k belongs to

l an explanation for
m live far (*incorrect answer had four words*)

Supplementary Activities

1

2 d **3** f **4** b **5** g **6** a **7** e

2

Possible answers
You should always listen to your friend's problems.
You must remember their birthday.
You don't have to share the same hobbies.
You mustn't tell them lies.
You shouldn't go out with their boyfriend/girlfriend.

Exam practice

1 did Anne leave
2 Do you like
3 comparison between
4 would not / wouldn't work
5 as hard as

Unit 4

1 *Possible answers*
just to talk to a friend; to complain about something; to tell some news; to ask for some information; to thank someone for something; to keep in touch; to give some information; to talk about how you're feeling etc.

2
2 f **3** g **4** b **5** l **7** k **8** n **9** a **10** c
11 j **12** e **13** i **14** m

3 *Possible answers*
 b Would you like to come to my party on Friday, 18th May?
 c Thanks a lot for a fantastic party.
 d (I) Hope everything is OK with your exam.
 e Don't forget to buy Mum's birthday present.
 f Has anyone seen my English book?
 g Ring David back as soon as possible.
 h I've just heard I've won a holiday to Barbados.

4 *Possible answers*

Example: Thanks a lot for …;   particularly the soup; What about meeting again soon? Are you free on Saturday 28th?
 a Stuart, would you like to come and stay this weekend? I know you're a football fan and there's a good football match on Saturday that we could go to. By the way, don't forget to bring your holiday photos – I really want to see them.

b Martina, I'm really sorry about your book. I had a cup of coffee on the table and I knocked it over with my elbow. But don't worry, I'll buy you another one at the weekend.

c Jon, thanks for looking after the fish. Can you feed them once a day – the fish food is on the table in the kitchen. I'll be back on Sunday but not until late so could you feed them on Sunday as well please?

Supplementary Activities

Possible answers

A Tony

There's been a change of plan. We're going to meet at the cinema at 7.30, not at the café. And Matt's not coming.

B Leo

Mohamed rang at 11.15. He wants you to ring him back as soon as possible. He's got some interesting news to tell you.

C Gina

That's wonderful news about the job. I'm really happy for you. How about meeting for dinner next week?

Unit 5

1

b CU = see you

c CU2nite = see you tonight

d CUL8r = see you later

e WerRU? = where are you?

f Wan2Tlk = want to talk?

g Thnx = thanks

2

Possible answers

Sorry I wasn't in when you called … shopping.
It's ages since our … remember?
Ring me back over … think.

3

Possible answers

I haven't written earlier … holiday.
It'll be very sad if your office closes *or* But maybe they haven't made the final decision yet.
It's very difficult when people … going on.

4

a Missing point: how long you'll be out (e.g. I'll be back about 7.)

b Extra information: So I'm going to college first to pick up my notes.

5

Possible answers

1 Oh dear! I lent your video to Barbara and I guess

she's still got it. She's mad about Buffy. Anyway, I enjoyed it very much. Would you like to borrow my Buffy 3 video for the weekend?
(Reply in student's own words)

2 Jaime, I'm moving to Milan in two months because of my Dad's job, so I'm not coming back to school next term. I don't want to go but I have to. Anyway, would you like to come and stay with me in Milan?
(Reply in student's own words)

Supplementary Activities

1 a When can I see you again?

b You do something to me.

c You blow my mind.

2 Three points:

- say where you are
- say what you're doing
- say what the best thing is

Exam practice

Possible answer

Congratulations! What wonderful news! Thank you for the invitation, I'd love to come to your engagement party. And how about meeting next week for lunch – say Wednesday? I'll give you a ring at the weekend to check.
See Appendix 1, page 114 for Students' sample answers.

Unit 6

1–2 *Student's own answers*

4

2 h **3** g **4** f **5** i **6** b **7** d **8** a **9** c

5

2 f **3** i **4** c **5** g **6** j **7** d **8** a **9** b **10** e

6 *Possible answer*

It's a modern apartment near the centre of the city and I really like it. It's on the tenth floor so we have great views. I live there with my family and I share a room with my brother. It's a bit small for the two of us – I'd like more space for all my things. The best room is the sitting room because it's big and you can walk out onto the balcony. We often have dinner there in the summer.

Supplementary Activities

Letter 1: f, d, h, b
Letter 2: c, g, a, e

Unit 7

1 *Possible answers*

b cooking
c a holiday
d my boss
e a particular club
f a car
g learning to snowboard
h scuba diving
i a computer system

See tapescript page 134 for sentences a–i.

2

2 got **3** 'm already planning **4** did **5** was
6 helped **7** went **8** was **9** 'll be **10** 'm staying
11 've just got **12** 'm going **13** seeing

3

1 f **2** e **3** c **4** a **5** d **6** b

See tapescript page 134 for complete letter.

4

(see Appendix 1 page 115 for students' sample answers)

Supplementary Activities

I'm looking forward to **seeing you** next week. Bring some warm clothes with **you because it's** still winter here, so you'll need them. And **of co**urse, don't forget to bring an umbre**lla and a wa**terproof jacket because it quite often **rains** in England! When you arrive at Heathrow, **go to the** coach station and catch the X90 – they lea**ve eve**ry hour and the journey takes about 00 **minutes**. It's a good idea to get a return ticket **because it's ch**eaper than two singles. Then, when you **arrive** in Oxford, ring me on your mobile and **I'll come** and pick you up at the coach station. **See you on** Saturday.

Unit 8

1 *Student's own answers*

2 *Possible answers*

a be able to get a good job
b learn another language
c get married
d move away from my town
e spend a year travelling
f learning to drive
g still have the same friends

3 *Possible answer*

Dear Charlotte
I've just come back from my holiday in Cuba. I really enjoyed it, especially the swimming. The sea was so warm and clear and you could see lots of fish. I spent hours in the water.
I think I'll go to Greece next year. A friend of mine went to Athens and said it was a great place. I'd really like to see some of the fantastic buildings there and then perhaps go to some of the islands for some more swimming. Why don't you come with me? It'll be fun together.
Anyway, I must stop now. Looking forward to seeing you on the 26th at Clare's party.
Love George

4

You asked me how I *usually* spend my summer holidays, and what I'm *planning* to do this year in July. I'm happy to tell you about this – it's something cheerful to think about now in *February*, when the *weather* is so cold and *miserable*. Do you remember I told you about my grandmother, who lives in the country on an old farm? Every summer we go there and spend four *wonderful* weeks riding horses, feeding the chickens and *swimming* in the lake. It's very cold water, but we still enjoy it. What are your plans for this summer? Looking forward to your next letter.

Best places to divide the letter are after 'miserable'. A new phase of the letter begins at this point. And after 'enjoy it' – the conclusion begins then.

5

Letter A

This letter answers the question – we know what her plans are. It takes a bit of time to get started and the ending is exactly the same wording as the question, so not appropriate. It is clearly organised with paragraphs. She uses a good variety of verb tenses, generally accurately. Vocabulary is OK – 'first trip'; 'my dream is'; 'within five years' but not ambitious. She shows control of the language but makes a number of errors. These errors do not stop the reader from understanding her message.

Letter B

This letter answers the question well. It has a clear beginning and ending and is well organised. The writer tries a variety of verb tenses but not always accurately ('I've received your letter yesterday'; 'if I will pass'; 'I'm not deciding.')
He tries to be ambitious with vocabulary but again, it doesn't always work well ('I'm in a particular moment', 'I must do my better'; 'How you can see

…'). His message is occasionally not clear because of errors like 'how' for 'as'.

(The authors think that both letters would be a 'Pass'.)

Supplementary Activities

1 *Student's own answers*

2 *Possible answer*

Thanks for your letter. My birthday was fun, but I didn't have a party this year. In the morning I went to my weight training class which is hard work, and then after I met Agnes (a friend from college) for a coffee in Blackwell's coffee shop. Later we both went shopping for some new trousers for me. I bought some black jeans, but when I got home I wasn't sure if I liked them really. In the evening, Sam and I went to see Monsoon Wedding at the cinema – it was brilliant, I really recommend it. And that was my birthday.
Love …

Unit 9

1 Picture a

3

2 c   3 a   4 f   5 b   6 e

(see tapescript for verb tenses in the story)

4 *Possible answers*

b was lying on the beach.

c saw the broken window.

d was working in the same office as me.

e she had made a mistake.

f when his computer began to make strange noises.

5 *Possible answers*

b She had arranged to meet her son and he was late.

c On Tuesday, Maria and I went to the opening of a new superstore in town.

d I was in the middle of nowhere and my car had broken down.

e It started badly when our plane was delayed for 12 hours.

6 *Students' own answers (See Appendix 1, page 115)*

Supplementary Activities

Student's own answers

Unit 10

1 *Possible answers*

Unfortunately, it was the wrong one.
Fortunately, he saw a tourist information office.
Unfortunately, it was closed.
Fortunately. he was able to ask someone in the street.
Unfortunately, this person was a stranger in the city etc.

2 a Marta was tired but got up early.
Marta was tired because she got up early.
Marta got up early so she was tired.

b Adam decided to go for a walk because it was warm.
Although it was warm, Adam decided to go for a walk.
It was warm but Adam decided to go for a walk.

3
b, h, f, a, e, g, i, d

4
b I burnt the toast so the smoke alarm went off.

c I had a row with my father as soon as he came/had come downstairs.

d I spilt my coffee while I was talking on the phone.

e I couldn't watch TV because I'd broken the remote control.

f I played on the computer until my brother wanted to use it.

g I had a row with my mother before she went to bed.

h It was a terrible day although Tuesday was even worse!

5
Possible answer

One cold winter evening, Andrea was sitting at home watching TV. There was an interesting programme on about Australia. Andrea thought 'I'd love to go there for a holiday,' so she decided to ring her friend, Tina, who lived in Sydney.
Two weeks later, Andrea was sitting on the plane on the way to Australia. The flight didn't seem too long because she enjoyed talking to the man next to her. After they arrived in sunny Sydney, Andrea walked into the arrivals area and saw Tina waiting. She didn't notice that her bag was open and her wallet had gone. Fortunately, the man from the plane picked it up and gave it back to her, so her holiday began well.

Supplementary Activities

Possible answers

On Monday it was raining so I decided not to go out.
On Tuesday, because it was snowing, I decided to go skiing.
On Wednesday the weather was very cold.
Unfortunately, I didn't have a warm jacket.
On Thursday it was foggy. Fortunately, the fog disappeared in the afternoon.
On Friday, although it was so windy, I sat in the park.
On Saturday suddenly the sun appeared and it was warm for a few hours.

Exam practice

Student's own answer

LISTENING

Unit 1

1

b 80   **c** 26   **d** 38 minutes   **e** 6 kilometres   **f** 2000
g 1489   **h** £2.81   **i** 30 cms   **j** 79%   **k** 382,650

2

a 80   **b** 6 hours   **c** 6 kms   **d** 30 cms   **e** £2.81
f 79%   **g** 26   **h** 382,650   **i** 1489   **j** 38 minutes
k 2000

3 a 1992   **b** 50   **c** 6   **d** June 14th
   e 9.30 am–3.00 pm   **f** 300 euros   **g** 50 euros

4 a Yes   **b** No   **c** No   **d** 22nd

5 a Yes   **b** No   **c** Yes   **d** train

6 *Possible answer*
   What sport does the woman play now?

7 Students draw a picture of an elephant.

8 Students write times – 2.00; 5.15; 4.00; 5.15 is correct answer.

9 A briefcase   B kitchen table   C chair
   Chair is correct answer.

Supplementary Activities

Student's own answers

Unit 2

1 a thunder   **b** clouds   **c** breeze   **d** pours
   e shines   **f** ice   **g** warm   **h** windy   **i** heat

2 a wind   fog   sun   rain
   b 2 grandfather   3 mother   4 daughter
     5 parents   6 cousins   7 uncle
   c legs   brushing   hair   a bath   bark

3

Rec 1: going shopping
Rec 2: where to meet
Rec 3: finding out about a concert
Rec 4: She dropped a glass and it broke.
     … fell out of my …
     … pieces of glass (on) the floor
Rec 5: (the end of) a film
     the screen   the lights

4

Rec 6: traditional; view of mountains; balconies
Rec 7: tall; curly hair; wears glasses; wears jeans

Supplementary Activities

One picture could show man washing up.
Another picture could show man reading a cookbook.
Correct picture shows man cooking (surrounded by mess).

Exam practice

1 C   **2** A   **3** C   **4** C   **5** C   **6** A   **7** B

Unit 3

1

1 heat   **2** hot   **3** hat   **4** height
5 heart   **6** hut   **7** hurt   **8** hit
Hut: The climbers stayed in a mountain **hut** overnight before starting their journey early the next morning.

2

a I've been walking all morning
b I'm going to live there
c What was she doing
d We saw the men outside the station
e The championship medal was won
f It's terrible that tigers are still shot
g It was a horrible taste
h Please heat the dessert
i What made her sink so fast
j She likes peas
k Is there a spare seat anywhere?
l Could you wash the baby please?

3

facilities   member   children   tennis courts
café   fun   get fit
four words
a last week **b** No **c** 6 indoor tennis courts
d 6.30 am–10.30 pm **e** a bar, a café, a car park
f bus or tram

4 a B **b** B **c** A **d** B **e** B **f** A

Unit 4

1 a ✗ **b** ✗ **c** ✓ **d** ✗ **e** ✗ **f** ✓

2

a High Street **b** small **c** eggs
d university students **e** Grand Café **f** small
g people in their 20s and 30s **h** mirrors on walls
i big **j** people of all ages **k** city centre
l quick snacks **m** it's outside **n** big
o groups of friends **p** live music

3

a a huge; breakfast
b looks much bigger; not cheap
c stay all day; talk about; have a coffee
d special; city centre; popular; pop in
e like a church; not so much; but the fact.

4 1 B **2** B **3** A **4** B **5** C

Supplementary Activities

Differences between two pictures:
lion on backpack
number of buttons on woman's shirt
bird on ground
menu cards
man wearing glasses
man reading/drinking
newspaper on table behind

Unit 5

1 a A **b** C (about 14m) **c** B (Russia 1st then
Canada) **d** B **e** A (the Japanese invented it)
f C (Nile, Amazon) **g** A

2 *Possible answers*
  b the crowds/the number of tourists
  c they are all different
  d the old city
  e rainy/wet/raining
  f sit and watch the activity in the harbour

3

a the main actress (Judy Garland)
b the length
c happy/good to be alive
d it's quite slow
e it's not as good
f C **g** A **h** C **i** B **j** C **k** C

Supplementary Activities

a on **b** director; actor **c** box office **d** screen
e scene **f** plays **g** ending
h comedy; action; thriller

Exam practice

1 B **2** C **3** B **4** A **5** B **6** C

Unit 6

1

a Gill Kenworthy **b** Juxon **c** refer; madam (both
words spell the same backwards and forwards)
d TTYL (talk to you later); HAND (have a nice day)

2

Which caller
    apologises for a mistake?   2
    asks Carole to ring back?   2, 4
    is a family member?   5
    invites Carole to something? 3
    talks about holiday plans?   1

Message 1: Out and About; 9.30; BBC2
Message 2: Mark; Tuesday; ring him
Message 3: a party; 24th; 112 Lexington Drive
Message 4: Tuesday at 8.10; tickets; £10–£45; ring
        her on 08766 327714
Message 5: David; Mum & Dad's Christmas present;
        write down ideas

4

2 Thatcher **3** RY/37590 **4** Grand Hotel
6 August **8** 10 days **9** write

Supplementary Activities

Possible answers

gate	tale	meal	same	gas	mat	lot
game	tail	mail	seal	get	sit	oil
gale	time	male	some	got	sat	ale
goal	tame	meat	late	toe	set	aim
goat	team	mate	item	met	let	age

Unit 7

3

1 38 **2** divorced **3** builder
4 climbing, sailing & fishing **5** listening to people
6 (being with) boring people
fitness rating – 4

4

1 £12m	**2** 88kph	**3** November 3rd
4 food	**5** 089705 200606	**6** £1m
7 50 seconds	**8** £18	**9** advance
10 Wardley		

Supplementary Activities

Student's own answers

Exam practice

1 13 **2** 50 metres **3** father **4** job
5 Saturday(s) **6** fish **7** 21

Unit 8

2

a Jenny **b** Jack **c** Marcus **d** Rob **e** Zoe **f** Renate

3

Rob: collecting stamps; *key words* – special books, ones with flowers on, envelopes and postcards, countries all over the world

Renate: a colleague; *key words* – boss, colleagues, computer, another department

Marcus: a pen; *key words* – biros, ink cartridges, moved so smoothly across the page

Zoe: neighbours; *key words* – apartment 22 and 23, hearing my music through the walls

Jack: a book; *key words* – reading, the shelf

4

a Yes **b** No **c** Yes **d** No **e** No **f** Yes **g** No
h Yes **i** No **j** Yes **k** Yes **l** No

5

Possible answers

Conversation 2: The man didn't enjoy the film.	Yes
The man didn't like anything in the film.	No
Conversation 3: The boy's grandma enjoys different kinds of music.	Yes
The boy's grandma is playing the Beatles.	No
Conversation 4: The man doesn't spend a lot of money on jeans.	Yes
The man thinks expensive jeans are better.	No

Supplementary Activities

1

a shy **b** cheerful **c** clever **d** honest
e relaxed **f** funny **g** friendly **h** generous

3

mean/generous stupid/clever sad/cheerful

Unit 9

2

a bet I won't **b** can't wait
c you should stay **d** have to work
e Let's go and
1 d **2** e **3** a **4** c **5** b

3

a	think about	No	Yes
b	didn't have to	Yes	No
c	would you	No	Yes

4

a	Is Martina interested in the sports programme on TV?	Yes
b	Does Martina feel unhappy about some animals living in cages?	Yes
c	Does Alex think it is necessary to keep animals in cages?	No
d	Does Martina already know something about Woburn?	Yes
e	Does Martina think that your car can be damaged if you visit Woburn?	Yes
f	Does Alex agree with Martina that some things about the park are quite funny?	No
g	Does Martina think the weather is right for this kind of trip?	No
h	Is the final decision OK for both speakers?	Yes

Supplementary Activities

Student's own answers – possible categories: land/sea/water/ number of legs/ domestic or wild/ useful or not useful/ carry things or not, etc.

Exam practice

1 Yes **2** No **3** No **4** Yes **5** No **6** Yes

SPEAKING

Unit 1

2   **Student A**: a **h**air b **a**ppointment c **n**ose
               d **i**nteresting e **c**ountry   = China

               a **e**lephant b **y**ear c **g**uilty d **m**ind
               e **a**unt f **r**ing g **N**ovember   = Germany

   Student B: a **i**nformation b **e**mpty c **c**ost
               d **x**-ray e **m**istake f **o**cean = Mexico

               a **L**isbon b **d**irty c **e**arly d **n**iece
               e **n**avy f **g**rapes g **a**lphabet = England

Football was first played in 200 BC in China.

A kind of basketball was common in Mexico in 10th century BC.

Bowling was played in Germany in the 17th century.

Baseball was first written about in 1700 in England.

5   2   Where are you from?
    3   What do you do?
    4   Have you travelled to any other countries?
    5   Where would you like to travel to in the future?
    6   Tell me something about your family

Topics covered: job/studies; family; travel; her future

6   *Student's own answers*

Exam practice

Student's own answers

Unit 2

1–3 *Student's own answers*

4   a   ✓ retired married couple.
    b   ✓ sentences 1, 3, 4, 5

5–6 *Student's own answers*

Unit 3

2   a   Shall I start?
    b   Who's going to start?
    c   Shall we start with this one? (✓)
    d   Would you like to begin? (✓)
    e   I'll go first.

3   a   What about this one?   b   What do you think about this one?   c   What do you think we should choose?   d   Why don't we choose a cheaper one?
    e   I think we should choose this one, don't you?
    f   Do you think this is a good one?

5   a   Who's going to start?   b   That's true; Yes, but; I agree; I think so too   c   We have to make a decision. Let's go for …   d   *Student's own answers*   e   yes, both did   f   equal speaking time   g   all 6 ideas

Supplementary Activities

Student's own answers

Unit 4

1

2   **Student A** *Possible answers*

a   There's a bookcase next to the door.
b   There's a picture on the wall, on the right of the bookcase.
c   The rug is on the floor in front of the sofa.
d   There are some magazines on the floor under the table.
e   The clock is above the door.
f   There's a vase on the bookcase.

   Student B *Possible answers*

a   The sofa is next to the table.
b   There's a lamp on the table.
c   The TV is in front of the sofa.
d   The videos are on (top of) the TV.
e   The remote control is on the sofa between the woman and the boy.

3   *Possible answers*

Photo A

I can see a family playing a game.

The boy is lying on the floor in front of the sofa.

They're holding cards in their hands.

The man is moving something.

The woman is smiling.

Two of them are wearing shorts.

Photo B

There are a lot of people having lunch or dinner.
They are sitting outside.
Nobody is eating at the moment.
Most of the men are wearing dark suits.
Some waiters are serving at the tables.
There's a boat coming up the river.

4 **a** hair **b** skin **c** look **d** is **e** clothes
f years old **g** fat **h** short **i** good

Pictures 3 and 5 ticked
Possible answers

Picture 1

In this picture, there's a woman lying down. She's got long dark hair and she's smiling. She's wearing a pink T-shirt. She's probably about 30.

Picture 2

In this picture there's a man. He's got dark hair and a beard. He's wearing a dark blue sweater. And in his hands he's got a small book. I guess he's about 30 or 35.

Picture 4

In this picture I can see a boy and he's sitting down. He's quite young and he's got dark curly hair. He's got a ball in his hands and he's looking at the floor. He's wearing jeans and a T-shirt.

Picture 6

In this picture I can see a man. He's got white hair, but not much of it, and he's also got a moustache. He's quite old – maybe about 70. He's wearing glasses and he's smiling. His hands are behind his head. He's wearing a blue shirt.

5 *Possible answers*
a You put a letter inside it. (envelope)
b It's a thing you use when you've cut yourself. (plaster)
c They're things for putting in your ears. (earrings)
d You use them for cutting something. (scissors)
e It's a thing for lighting a room. (candle)
f It's something you use when you want your eyes to look good. (mascara)
g It's a thing for writing. (pencil)
h You use it to put your CDs in. (CD tower)
i It's a thing you use when you're cooking. (pan)

Supplementary Activities

Possible answers
boots, bikini; coat, cap; dress; earrings; fleece; glasses, gloves; hat, helmet; jeans, jacket, jumper, knickers; nightdress; pyjamas, pants; raincoat; socks, shoes; trousers, trainers; underwear; vest, v-neck sweater; waistcoat, watch

Unit 5

1 **b** She looks as if she's going to cry. **c** It looks hot. **d** It looks like summer. **e** He looks like his father. **f** They don't look happy. **g** It doesn't look as if anyone is living there. **h** It looks empty.

2 *Student's answers*
a pencils **b** a CD
c the bottom of a glass **d** drops of water

3 *Possible answers*
Photo B
They look relaxed.
It looks like winter because they're wearing warm clothes.
Perhaps they are husband and wife.
They might be discussing something because they look quite serious.
I think it's a big town because I can see some big buildings in the background.
Perhaps they've just had lunch and they need a walk after it.
It's probably quite cold because she's wearing a hat and scarf.

Photo A
It looks lovely.
It looks like summer because the sky is blue.
They look as if they're exploring the area in their boats.
They might be on holiday.
I think they're enjoying themselves because it looks fun.
Perhaps they are all friends.
It's probably a river or a lake.

5 *Possible answer*
Both students give good answers but the first student gives a better description. He includes place, action, something about the people, his impressions and opinions and he doesn't get worried about the things in the people's hands.

The second student includes place, action and a lot on what people are wearing.
Two suggestions to make the second description better:
Talk about impressions more e.g. the people listening look cold so it might be wintertime.
I don't think they look very happy. The people playing the music are probably hoping for money etc.
Don't spend time trying to think of particular vocabulary.

Supplementary Activities

Possible answers

Facts

- A woman is carrying two yellow bags.
- There are a lot of bright colours.
- It's a street market.
- I can't see any cars or other traffic.
- A woman is carrying a baby on her front.

Impressions

- It looks like a Far East country.
- I think it's a warm place.
- It doesn't look very busy.
- It's probably a cheap place to shop.
- They look as if they've done most of their shopping.

Unit 6

1 *Possible answers*

a Where do you live?
b Do you like your job?
c When did you start playing the guitar?
d What do you do in your free time?
e What kind of music do you like?
f Who's your favourite musician?
g Do you go out shopping a lot?
h How long are you going to stay in Italy?
i What do you think of Italy?
j Have you been to Italy before?
k What would you like to do in the future?

2 *Possible answers*

Student A

a What kind of music do you enjoy?
b When you were younger did you like the same kind of music?
c Who's your favourite band or singer now?
d Who was your favourite band or singer when you were younger?
e How often do you listen to music?
f Do you like going to concerts?
g Can you play an instrument?

Student B

a What kind of food do you eat at home?
b Do you enjoy going to restaurants?
c What's your favourite food?
d Is there anything that you don't like?
e How often do you go to a restaurant?
f What do you usually eat at lunchtime?
g What did you have for dinner last night?
h Can you cook?

3 *Student's own answers – Possible answers*

I really like watching football (because it's exciting).
I can't stand eating outside (because I don't like insects).
I love surfing the net (because I learn lots of new things).
I'm not very keen on watching videos (because I'd prefer to go to the cinema).
I don't mind rain (because we don't get it very often).
I quite like shopping (because I like clothes).

Supplementary Activities

1

a How often do you go to the cinema?
b Who are you going out with tonight?
c How long have you had a car?
d Which university do you want to study at?
e Have you always been interested in cooking?

2 *Student's own answers*

GRAMMAR FILE

Exercise 1
2 know 3 don't want 4 get 5 have 6 am doing
7 spend 8 always go 9 are getting 10 aren't working

Exercise 2
2 heard 3 sounded 4 ran 5 looked
6 were shouting 7 were laughing 8 understood
9 was happening 10 were waiting

Exercise 3
b discovered c had never eaten d had stopped
e relaxed f had forgotten g was

Exercise 4
b since c for d since e since f Since g for
h for

Exercise 5
b haven't decided c Has (he) ever bought d hasn't finished e has just lost f have never heard g Have you played h have already gone

Exercise 6
b I've never been c Mika met; went (✓) d (✓) e haven't eaten f Did you see; I have seen

Exercise 7
b are; were/are c is d am e was f are g were
h make/ manufacture; sell i breaks

Exercise 8
Student's own answers with *(not) going to* (a–e) and *will* (*'ll*) (f–k)

Exercise 9 (*Possible answers*)
b What are you doing for your summer holidays this year? **c** What time is Paul meeting us?
d Sonia can't … because she's babysitting tonight.
e Zoe is having a party on Saturday for her birthday.
f Our next-door neighbours are moving next month.
g How many people are coming to dinner tonight?
h Are you working at the weekend?

Exercise 10 (*Possible answers*)
b … today I've decided to go by car. **c** … it was extremely expensive, **d** … I took my jacket off.
e … he played very well. **f** … everybody knows what you're doing. **g** … he's very strong. **h** … I left early.
i … we decided to go for a walk. **j** … he sang in the shower.

Exercise 11
b As soon as/When **c** after/when/as soon as
d while/when **e** until/before **f** when/after/as soon as
g until **h** until; before **i** After/When/As soon as
j before/when

Exercise 12
a … the biggest city **b** … not as old as Marc **c** ✓
d … is a better skier **e** … to be less snow than
f … are warmer **g** … one of the most difficult **h** … is more beautiful than
Possible answers
i … as good at sport as I was
j … much more adventurous than I am now
k … better at English than I used to be

Exercise 13
2 travelling **3** to go **4** to join **5** studying
6 to start **7** to camp **8** sleeping **9** to tell
10 to enjoy **11** coming **12** hearing

Exercise 14
Possible answers
1 It's definitely a hot country. It might be Spain. It's probably summertime. They might be husband and wife. Perhaps they're talking about where to go.
2 Perhaps it's in England. It might be winter. They're definitely brothers. They're probably talking about football.

Exercise 15
b should/ought to **c** don't have to/don't need to
d ought **e** should **f** must not **g** doesn't need to/doesn't have to **h** must **i** should

Exercise 16
Student's own answers

Exercise 17 *possible answers*
2 vegetables **3** bread **4** milk **5** apples **6** pears
7 cream **8** cheese **9** cauliflower **10** smoked salmon **11** ice cream

Exercise 18
a How <u>are you</u> feeling today? **b** <u>Did you</u> enjoy your visit … ? **c** What <u>are you</u> going to do …?
d How many brothers or sisters <u>have you got</u>?
e ✓ **f** Can you tell me how much <u>this costs</u>?
g Do you know <u>who I am</u>? **h** <u>Which is</u> the best restaurant in town? **i** <u>Are you going</u> to see … ?
j How many languages <u>can you</u> speak? *or* <u>do you</u> speak?

Exercise 19
a did you leave **b** We left **c** Are you **d** is still
e us to leave **f** our rooms were

Exercise 20
a Have you ever seen Mount Everest? **b** I'm just back from a trip to Peru. **c** When I arrive in a country I always hire a car.
d I'm going to Iceland next week. **e** Travelling is sometimes difficult if you don't speak the local language.
f I could only stay in Italy for one day. **g** I often stay with friends in Quebec. **h** I'm still hoping to see the Leaning Tower of Pisa. **i** I've never visited Bhutan.
j Last summer I spent two weeks in China. **k** I usually fly first class when I travel abroad. **l** I'm already planning my next trip to Bolivia.
The two countries are: Turkey and Canada

PRACTICE TEST

Paper 1 Reading

Part 1
1 B **2** A **3** C **4** B **5** C

Part 2
6 F **7** B **8** D **9** G **10** A

Part 3
11 A **12** A **13** A **14** B **15** A
16 B **17** A **18** B **19** B **20** A

Part 4
21 C **22** D **23** D **24** A **25** B

Part 5
26 C **27** C **28** A **29** B **30** B
31 D **32** C **33** B **34** B **35** D

Writing

Part 1
1 has (got)/contains more 2 are/feel/get tired
3 unless 4 haven't bought
5 too expensive

Part 2
Question 6 – *student's own answers*

Part 3
Questions 7 and 8 – *student's own answers*

Paper 2 Listening

Part 1
1 B 2 A 3 C 4 C 5 B 6 C 7 B

Part 2
8 B 9 A 10 B 11 C 12 C 13 B

Part 3
14 Nigeria 17 brother
15 economics 18 85
16 teacher 19 £18m

Part 4
20 B 21 A 22 B 23 A 24 B 25 B

Acknowledgements

The authors and publishers would like to thank the teachers and students who trialled and commented on the material:

Argentina: Maria Silvia Laclau; Cyprus: Peter Lucantoni; France: Alison Maillard, Robert Wright; Italy: Tim Julian, Paul Rogerson; Malta: Greg Burrell; Mexico: Roger Brooks, Bronwen Davies, Jan Isaksen; Spain: Henny Burke, Jake Haymes, Samantha Lewis, Nick Shaw, Brendan Smith, Chris Turner; Switzerland: Julia Muller, Jean Rüdiger-Harper, Fiona Schmid; UAE: Philip Lodge; UK: David Barrett, Ann Doherty, Lynda Edwards, Joe Gillespie, Mary Scharnhorst, Roger Scott, Clare West, Norman Whitby, Lizzie Wright; US: Gregory Manin.

The authors would like to thank Rawdon Wyatt for inspiring them to write the jumbled letters multiple-choice activity in exercise 6 on page 25, a form of which appeared in *First Certificate Games & Activities*, published by Penguin.

The authors and publishers are grateful to the following for permission to use copyright material in *Insight into PET*. While every effort has been made, it has not been possible to identify the sources of all the material used and in such cases the publishers would welcome information from the copyright owners:

For the article SOS Shark rescue, p. 18, Merlin Entertainments Group Limited. www.sealife.co.uk; 'Experience Africa' p. 19, by kind permission of *BBC Wildlife Magazine*; 'Why eating chocolate is good for you', p. 20, first published in the *Daily Mail*, 28 August 2000 © Atlantic Syndication Limited; 'From sweaty socks to lifestyle choice', p. 21, first published in *The Independent*, 22 April 2001 © Independent Newspapers; 'Gym brands part 2' by Andrew Hamilton on p. 23, published in *Ultra-FIT magazine* Vol.12 no.2 © Ultra-FIT Publications Ltd; for the article on p. 25, adapted from 'I grew up with lions in my living room' by Maisie McNiece, published in *Cosmogirl*, May 2002 © The National Magazine Company Limited; for the article on p. 26, adapted from 'When I was 12' published in *Mizz*, 6 March 2002 © IPC Media; for the article on p. 31, 'An unusual place to live', adapted from 'The jet settler', published in the *Cover Magazine*, March 1999, the Mirror Group © Trinity Mirror Plc; for the article, 'Two rides' on p. 71,

adapted from 'Flying High', with kind permission of the Author, Laura Barton, published in *The Guardian*, 13 April 2002; for the 'Dance Marathon' story in Unit 5 of the audio recording, adapted from 'Endurance Test' in '*Did you know*,' by permission of The Reader's Digest Association Limited © 1990.

The publishers are grateful to the following for permission to include photographs:

Alamy Images/Mark Lewis, p. 70; Alton Towers p. 71 (top left); Art Directors/TRIP pp. 23 /H Rogers, 38 /A Tovy, 39 /J Okwesa, 63/ H Rogers; John Birdsall Photography p. 97; J Bloxham p. 83 (top right); CeladorInternational Ltd p. 34; Corbis pp. 83 (top left) /Chris Carroll, 83 (bottom right) /Norbert Schaefer, 85 (left) / Michael Prince; Crown Decorative Products Ltd p. 83 (bottom left); Getty Images pp. 19 /Art Wolfe (left), 35; Image State p. 133 (right)/Donna Day; Instituto de Turismo de España p. 91 (bottom); Robert Harding Picture Library pp. 89 (bottom left), 101,133 (left); Ken Kerbs/DOT Pictures, USA p. 91 (top); Life File Photo Library pp. 85 (centre right) /Emma Lee, 85 (right)/Lionel Moss, 89 (top left) /Jeff Greenberg, 90 (bottom) /Graham Burns, 41 /Jeremy Hoare, 53 /Paul Fisher; Minden Pictures, California,USA/Frans Lanting p. 19 (centre left); Paul Mulcahy pp. 78, 96; Oxford Scientific Films p. 8 /Warren Faidley, 85 (centre left) /David M Dennis; Pictures Colour Library pp. 37, 54, 66; Popperfoto/Reuters pp. 21 (left) /Peter Nacduarnud, 48 /Pierre Tostee/ASP, 71 (bottom) /Fabrizio Bensch; Powerstock pp. 21 (right) /Rosenfeld, 65 /Sammy; Rex Features pp. 20 /Ray Tang, 24 /Steve Lyne 31 /Chris Bott, 44 /Tony Kyriacou, 56 /Michael Friedel, 83 (bottom centre /Julian Mackey; Anup Shah/Naturepl.com p. 19 (centre right & right); Seaco Picture Library p. 89 (top right); Sony Ericsson p. 90 (top); Lynn Stone /Naturepl.com p. 33; Thorpe Park p. 71 (top right); Chris Tubbs p. 89 (bottom (right); Jake Walters p. 83 (top centre).

Picture research by Valerie Mulcahy

Illustrations by Adrian Barclay, Colin Brown, John Dunn, Phil Gardner, Sharon Harmer, Bernice Lum, Ian West and Kamae Design